What Do Gay Men Want?

What Do Gay Men Want?

An Essay on
Sex, Risk, and Subjectivity

David M. Halperin

THE UNIVERSITY OF MICHIGAN PRESS • ANN ARBOR

First paperback edition 2009
Copyright © 2007 by David M. Halperin
All rights reserved
Published in the United States of America by
The University of Michigan Press
Manufactured in the United States of America
♾ Printed on acid-free paper

2012   2011   2010   2009   5   4   3   2

A CIP catalog record for this book is available from the British Library.

Library of Congress Cataloging-in-Publication Data

Halperin, David M., 1952–
   What do gay men want? : an essay on sex, risk, and
subjectivity / David M. Halperin.
        p.   cm.
   Includes bibliographical references.
   ISBN-13: 978-0-472-11622-5 (cloth : alk. paper)
   ISBN-10: 0-472-11622-3 (cloth : alk. paper)
   1. Gay men—Psychology.   2. Sex (Psychology)   3. Gay men—
Attitudes.   I. Title.

HQ76.H29   2007
306.76'62—dc22   2007019160

ISBN-13: 978-0-472-03365-2 (pbk. : alk. paper)
ISBN-10: 0-472-03365-4 (pbk. : alk. paper)

For
J / R / Z

Contents

What Do Gay Men Want?

I

What do gay men want?

According to a number of recent novels, gay men just want to be held. According to some current writing about HIV/AIDS prevention, gay men actually want to be killed. According to most critical work in queer studies—well, most critical work in queer studies has nothing to say about the subject.[1]

The silence of queer studies on the topic of gay male subjectivity—the inner life of male homosexuality, what it is that gay men want—is no accident. The Gay Liberation movement of the 1960s and 1970s may have had its ideological roots in a combination of Marxism and Freudianism, and it may have understood its struggles to be directed as much against psychic *re*pression as political *op*pression, but the kind of lesbian and gay studies that emerged in Great Britain and North America during the 1980s was largely uninterested in exploring questions of lesbian and gay male subjectivity. That is because subjectivity at the time tended to be understood in terms of psychology, and psychology had long represented a tainted category for lesbians, gay men, and other sexual dissidents.

For more than a century, any deviation from very strict standards of normative gender presentation and heterosexual behavior had been considered, and treated, as the sign of a psychological illness—as a symptom of a diseased state, variously described as "moral insanity," "sexual perversion," "personality disorder," "mental illness," or "maladjustment," but characterized in any case as a kind of abnormal psychology. Even as late as the 1970s and 1980s, many reputable psychiatrists and psychoanalysts continued to maintain in all seriousness that homosexuals were sick. And as recently as 1999, a prominent psychologist could speculate, in the pages of a scientific publication, that "homosexuality represents a deviation from normal development and is associated with other such deviations that may lead to mental illness."[2] In the wake of more than a century of medical and forensic treatment of homosexuality as a psychiatric pathology or aberration, lesbians and gay men of the post-Stonewall era directed much political effort to undoing the presumption that there was something fundamentally wrong with us. In this context, it seemed necessary to close off the entire topic of gay subjectivity to respectable inquiry, so as to prevent gayness from ever again being understood as a sickness.

In pursuit of that goal, the lesbian and gay movement has produced a remarkably plausible and persuasive new definition of homosexuality in political rather than psychological terms. To be gay, according to this new definition, is not to exhibit a queer subjectivity, but to belong to a social group. Homosexuality refers not to an individual abnormality but to a collective *identity*. Although on this view homosexuality may simply be a natural human variation, it has nevertheless been the object of social hostility, of intense and irrational prejudice, leading to widespread and unjustified discrimination against gay people. To be gay therefore is to be marked, through no fault of one's own, by the stigma that comes from persistent social rejection and exclusion. What gay people have in common, then, is not a psychological disorder but a social disqualification. We also share a long history of savage, even genocidal oppression, which gives us an immediate political claim to social tolerance, freedom from discrimination, and overall improvement in our life chances.

By virtue of being defined in this way, as members of a stigmatized group, but as otherwise no different from "normal people," lesbians and gay men have acquired a collective identity equivalent to that of any ethnic or religious group that is socially marked by its perceived difference from regular folks. Once lesbians and gay men succeeded in convincing both straight people and ourselves to view us in this way, with help from the precedent set by earlier campaigns against social stigma (notably, the Black Power movement and various third-world struggles for decolonization), we were able to achieve a certain degree of public acceptance as well as assimilation into society at large. So the practice of foregrounding gay identity and backgrounding gay subjectivity turned out to have a political payoff that we could not afford to despise. And it has also saved us from the persistent specter of psychopathology. We are still, understandably, reluctant to abandon that political strategy, and we get nervous when anyone departs from it.

🌸 *Another reason* why many practitioners of lesbian and gay studies nowadays tend to avoid the topic of gay subjectivity is that they are still heavily influenced by the work of Michel Foucault, a French philosopher and historian who was also a gay man. In the first volume of his *History of Sexuality,* originally published in 1976 and translated into English in 1978, Foucault advanced a powerful critique of sexual liberation. He argued, unexpectedly but persuasively, that the struggle against psychic repression, far from liberating sexual desire and leading to an overthrow of the régime of the normal, sometimes actually results in new and more insidious ways of naturalizing and enforcing sexual normality. For implicit in the revolutionary program of sexual liberation are a lot of unexamined, supposedly self-evident, but quite loaded and highly normative assumptions about what sexuality is, how it shapes human nature, and which are the most proper, healthy ways of expressing it.

In order to challenge those assumptions, Foucault elaborated a radically political approach to sexuality. He redefined sexuality as a necessary element internal to the functioning of the modern liberal state and its systems of power. Foucault's political understanding of sexuality emphasized the impersonal operation of discourses, institutions, and similar social practices, granting little salience to the workings of individual interiority and deliberately displacing rival approaches that located sexuality at the core of the human subject. With its emphasis on the social and political utility of sexuality for the governing of individuals, Foucault's startling take on sexuality proved to be well suited to the needs of gay and lesbian resistance in the 1980s, when the rise of the New Right and the emergence of the HIV/AIDS epidemic combined to devastate queer communities and to erase many of our hard-won social gains.

Foucault also offered the only theoretical approach to sexuality sufficiently substantive and original to compete with psychoanalysis—and to afford a meaningful intellectual alternative to it within the field of sexuality studies. Since psychoanalysis had long participated in the pathologizing of homosexuality, especially in the United States,[3] and since the re-pathologizing of homosexuality was precisely what lesbian/gay politics had to contend with during the onset of the HIV/AIDS pandemic, it is no wonder that so much early work in lesbian/gay studies and queer theory took its initial inspiration, and drew so many of its critical axioms, from Foucault.[4]

Another way of putting this point is to say that lesbians and gay men had lots of reasons independent of Foucault for not wanting to think about the distinctive properties of queer subjectivity. Given the long history of treating sexual differences not as benign variations but as diseases or abominations, it would be risky indeed to ascribe any particular subjective characteristics or practices to homosexuality, because any feature unique to the inner lives of lesbians or gay men would likely be interpreted as a symptom or expression of pathology. When Foucault declared in 1981 that "the entire art of life consists in killing off psychology" *(L'art de vivre, c'est de tuer la psychologie)*,[5] he was voicing an attitude common to many lesbians and gay men of his generation who, like him, had spent a lifetime struggling against their own sense of psychological deviance, while also trying to shrug off the unflattering judgments of psychological experts and to dodge the constant, perennial accusations of perversion, sickness, abnormality.

The problem with killing off psychology, though, was that for more than a hundred years psychology, and subsequently psychoanalysis, had provided the chief means of access to the imagined truth of human subjectivity. Killing off psychology in such a context meant foreclosing all access to the category of gay subjectivity itself, bracketing it as an object of gay investigation, and thereby making it impossible to ask, much less to answer, the question, "What do gay men want?" That, indeed, was precisely the point: to make the world safe for lesbians and gay men by focusing on the politically acceptable category of *gay identity* and by shifting attention away from the disquieting and potentially discreditable details of *gay subjectivity*. The aim was to distract straight people from everything about gay culture that might make them feel uncomfortable with it, suspicious of it, or excluded from it, and to get them to sympathize instead with our political (and therefore less viscerally upsetting) demands for equal treatment, social recognition, and procedural justice. Those are the sorts of demands, after all, that are most likely to be found reasonable by people who don't have especially warm feelings for gay people but who can be moved to tolerate us, or at least not to mistreat us, when one appeals to their basic sense of fairness and decency. Foreclosing the question of gay subjectivity was a small price to pay for scuttling a psychological model of homosexual difference premised on sexual abnormality and replacing it with a political program grounded in a non-psychological notion of gayness as a quasi-ethnic social identity.

A small price, then—but a necessary one? What if psychology were not the only means of access to the supposed truth of subjectivity? What if the psychic were not necessarily the royal road to knowledge of the internal workings of the gay subject? Even during the period of their ascendancy, psychology and psychoanalysis were shadowed by an alternate tradition, perhaps not a consistent tradition so much as a persistent impulse, visible conspicuously (though not exclusively) in the work of a number of gay male writers. In their different ways, Walter Pater, Oscar Wilde, André Gide, Marcel Proust, Jean Genet, and Roland Barthes all attempted to imagine and to represent human subjectivity without recourse to psychology.[6] And as Foucault's later work makes clear, Foucault himself was hardly trying to impose a blackout on all inquiry into "the hermeneutics of the subject": that, after all, was the title he gave to his lectures at the Collège de France in the winter and spring of 1982.[7] On the contrary, Foucault was challenging himself, and us, to find ways of approaching subjectivity that would not necessarily be routed through psychology or through the already familiar and increasingly trite conceptual categories of psychoanalysis.

❧ *To be sure,* Foucault had little to say, even in those 1982 lectures, about what an anti-psychological hermeneutics of the subject might look like. In fact, he had little to say about any kind of interpretative or explanatory model of the subject. Despite the title he came up with for his course, Foucault decided to approach the relations between the subject and truth—his principal topic—via a study of the theory and the practice of the "care of the self" in Hellenistic and Roman philosophy some two thousand years earlier. Foucault chose to focus on that distant, transitional period in the history of Western thought precisely because, according to him, a hermeneutics of the subject in the modern sense was strikingly, tellingly absent from it. In other words, it was because the subject's relation to truth in the philosophical discourses of the time did *not* take the form of a psychological discipline of introspection and decipherment—of an actual "hermeneutics"—that Foucault decided to examine it so closely. In place of a modern science of the subject that treats the self as a locus of psychological depth, the site of an interiority which it is crucial to explore and to chart (so as to distinguish normal kinds of mental functioning from their perverted opposites), Foucault wanted to advance "an analytics of the forms of reflexivity . . . that constitute the subject as such."[8] Foucault, then, was concerned almost entirely with the techniques of self-fashioning—and with the different kinds of subjects that different kinds of relations to oneself could produce. He presented those techniques of self-fashioning as a historical alternative to, if not quite the antithesis of, the practices of self-analysis familiar to us from Christian and Freudian culture. He even acknowledged as much, emphasizing in his published summary of the course in the *Annuaire* of the Collège de France that the Greek and Roman "culture of the self" he had described in his lectures was "still very far away from what would [later] be a hermeneutics of the subject."[9]

Nonetheless, in a number of Foucault's passing remarks in his 1982 lectures on the differences between ancient self-knowledge, on the one hand, and Christian and Freudian self-exegesis, on the other, we can begin to glimpse the outlines of a possible non-disciplinary hermeneutics of the subject. They emerge from Foucault's strenuous efforts to define a historical form of the relations between the subject and truth that would offer an alternative to modern methods of mapping and analyzing psychic interiority and would represent a practice of self-knowledge opposed, or at least opposable, to more recent Christian and Freudian techniques.[10] Foucault was at pains to recover and to describe a model of knowing the self that had been prominent in the past, that was distinct from "the sciences of the mind, psychology, the analysis of consciousness," and that did not lie at their origin.[11] Over against "the objectification [*l'objectivation*] of the self in a true discourse," characteristic both of Christianity and psychology, the ancient "culture of the self" afforded a radically different possibility: "the subjectivation of a true discourse in a practice and exercise of oneself on oneself."[12]

Foucault argued that this non-exegetical mode of knowing the self, though largely neglected by modern philosophy and culture in the West, had never completely died out. Indeed, "a whole section of nineteenth-century thought can be reread as a difficult attempt, a series of difficult attempts, to reconstitute an ethics and an aesthetics of the self."[13] In the interviews he gave to the gay press at about the same time as he was delivering those lectures, Foucault made it clear that he saw the promise of the lesbian and gay movement in a similar light. Queer politics was a way of killing off psychology and of reactivating an ethics of the self that would consist not in self-analysis, nor in adherence to norms of proper, healthy functioning, but in "an aesthetics of existence."[14] Foucault found in certain modes of queer life new possibilities for self-fashioning and self-knowledge. Although those queer ways of life might be very different from the ancient practices of the self with which Foucault was concerned in his scholarly work, they resembled their ancient forebears insofar as they offered an alternative to the scientific and normative disciplines of the self favored by our post-Christian, post-Freudian culture. At least, that was the radical hope Foucault glimpsed in the lesbian and gay movement.

❧ *If we are* to keep that hope alive, we will have to forge queer alternatives to the modern, scientific culture of the self and its psychological hermeneutics of the subject. Queer culture has in fact shown itself to be prolific in inventing concrete escape-routes from self-analysis, ranging from gay churches to gay bathhouses.[15] And a number of gay male writers, as I mentioned, have already elaborated various anti-psychological approaches to representing the queer subject. So queer people have a multitude of both social and intellectual resources to draw on when it comes to figuring out how to have a subjectivity, and a sexual subjectivity in particular, without conceptualizing or experiencing it in terms of either psychology or psychoanalysis.

For that is indeed the major challenge we face nowadays when we try to think about subjectivity, sexuality, truth, and power after Foucault. It is less a question of coming up with new theories of sexuality than of mobilizing queer possibilities for imagining and representing the subjective life of sex—the subjective life of homosexuality, most specifically—and, if necessary, freeing ourselves from the authority of Theory and from the doctrinaire and scientistic limitations it now imposes on what can be said and thought.[16] It is not a matter of refuting or rejecting psychoanalysis outright, nor of condemning and demonizing the academic field of Psychology as a whole—which, after all, includes the radical subfields of social psychology and critical psychology, so useful for documenting collective practices and formations of subjectivity and for locating in subjectivity itself a potential site of political resistance.[17] It is rather a matter of challenging the pervasive culture of psychology in modernity, the popular practices and discourses of psychology (that is, psychology with a small *p*), along with their disciplinary, academic base in depth psychology, personality psychology, the psychological sciences of the individual.[18] The goal is not to discredit psychology as an intellectual project so much as to escape a style of thinking that understands the person in terms of individual interiority and judges subjective life according to a normative standard of healthy functioning.

That will not be easy. The specialized, conceptual languages of psychology and psychoanalysis have been elaborated over more than a century. They provide a systematic, complex, comprehensive, and authoritative vocabulary for representing mental processes. No other languages for mapping the inner worlds of human beings can now rival them in descriptive or analytical power (the languages of Christian spirituality once came very close). But that is the problem. The highly developed theoretical and methodological state of psychology and psychoanalysis leaves the false impression that they are true, that the terms in which they are couched are in a relation of one-to-one correspondence with the mental processes they purport to represent. Even worse, it gives rise to a kind of linguistic and conceptual monoculture, in which there is but a single viable vocabulary for describing our subjective worlds. The overall effect is to make us feel that other ways of talking about ourselves are hopelessly impressionistic, lacking in rigor, unable to compete with those sciences, or to give us meaningful access to our inner lives.

And yet, there is good reason to believe that the languages of psychology and psychoanalysis are not necessarily the right ways or the best ways to talk about our subjective existence. When, for example, it comes to capturing the experiences of loss, grief, and mourning—or desire, attachment, and love—the languages of psychology and psychoanalysis are notoriously impoverished, awkward, mechanical, imprecise, inadequate.[19] We need, in addition to them, other ways of being able to speak about ourselves, about our experiences, about our emotions, and, in particular, about the subjective life of sex and sexuality.

Queer culture already offers us some of the alternatives we need. We just have to learn how to recognize, how to value, and how to champion the queer cultural traditions that have come down to us. Those traditions provide us with eloquent examples of how to think about sexuality beyond and outside of psychoanalysis—and how to think about sexual subjectivity without psychology. Queer thought may not have the same sheen of scientific objectivity or sophistication as psychology or psychoanalysis. In fact, it may seem utterly laughable as science. But that, in our current context at least, is entirely to its advantage.

Or so I hope to show in what follows.

II

If there was ever any doubt about the urgent political need to find ways of representing gay male subjectivity without necessary or automatic recourse to psychology and psychoanalysis, the merest glance at contemporary discourses about why some gay men have risky (or "unsafe") sex would dispel it. The topic of gay men's sexual risk-taking has opened new perspectives onto gay male subjectivity and occasioned a multitude of inquiries—by scientists, journalists, community leaders, and activists—into what gay men want. Nearly all of those inquiries have taken the form of psychological speculation about gay men's motives for engaging in risky sex. That speculation has led in turn to a revival of medical thinking about homosexuality: a style of reasoning that distinguishes "healthy" from "unhealthy" behavior, and thereby tends to smuggle into an ostensibly scientific analysis many stealth assumptions about good and bad sex, functional and dysfunctional subjectivity, proper and improper human subjects. Starting from the premise that no sane person would ever put his life at risk to obtain sexual pleasure—a dubious premise at best, which acquires a specious plausibility by being grounded in unexamined normative notions about psychological health—most efforts to understand gay men's sexual risk-taking complicate their task by setting themselves the impossible goal of explaining behavior that has already been defined as deeply irrational or incomprehensible.

The causes of such behavior then tend to be sought in various psychological "deficits" that impair gay men's mental health and interfere with normal functioning.

Some of this speculation aims to be gay-friendly: it portrays gay men as victims of hostile social forces, diagnoses the various ills from which we suffer as a consequence, and offers to help us into recovery by providing therapeutic remedies for the damage we have sustained. Other accounts are more straightforwardly homophobic. But whatever the intention, the result is to portray gay men as beset by a number of serious psychological conditions, ranging (on the "victim" end of the scale) from internalized homophobia, survivor guilt, and post-traumatic stress disorder to (on the pathological end) low self-esteem,[20] addictive personality syndrome, sexual compulsiveness, and lack of self-control.

It is not clear exactly how many gay men engage in sex that carries a real risk of transmitting HIV, how many of us take what kinds of risks, to what extent we succeed in minimizing those risks, or what the demographic distribution of gay risk-takers is, either in the United States or around the world. Formal monitoring of the HIV/AIDS epidemic has often been spotty or inconsistent, especially in the United States, where the Centers for Disease Control and Prevention did not receive confidential name-based reporting of cases of HIV infection from New York until 2000; California began for the first time to furnish the CDC with such information in April 2006, while Illinois, Massachusetts, and nine other states, plus the District of Columbia (with the highest AIDS prevalence rate in the nation), have yet to provide the CDC with such statistically useful, though socially sensitive, data.[21] Even the most sophisticated statistical analyses of gay men's risk-taking tend to be based on partial, incomplete, unrepresentative, or flawed information.

Nonetheless, certain consistent patterns have emerged. David Nimmons, who surveyed more than sixty behavioral studies published during the 1990s, reports that "the proportion of [gay] men primarily behaving safely [which means different things in different studies, but tends to equate somewhat misleadingly with using condoms] commonly hovers between 60 and 70 percent"; by contrast, the percentage of heterosexual women and men practicing safe sex rarely attains a third of the sample.[22] Those percentages are not in themselves reliable indicators of actual risk, however, because not all *unprotected* (i.e., condomless) sex is necessarily *unsafe* sex.[23] Unprotected sex cannot enable the transmission of HIV unless it takes place between an infected and an uninfected partner, and even then the exact degree of risk involved depends on the specific sexual acts performed and a complex array of secondary factors.[24] In any case, what does seem to be clear is that only a fairly small minority of self-identified gay men in the industrialized world currently put themselves at significant risk of contracting HIV/AIDS in their sexual practices.[25]

To be sure, the last decade *has* witnessed a growing alarm in both popular and scientific circles about increased sexual risk-taking by gay men. The production of panic scenarios about gay men's sexual behavior in the context of the HIV/AIDS epidemic is of course nothing new, but a number of recent developments have provided a fresh motive for particular concern. Chief among them is the emergence of "barebacking," the deliberate, premeditated practice of unprotected anal sex with casual or anonymous partners,[26] which has garnered considerable attention from journalists and epidemiologists alike. Still, there is reason to believe that barebacking, however worrisome, does not represent the terrifying menace to public health that some have taken it to be. By saying this I do not mean to minimize the gravity of the situation. Concerns about a rise in risky sex among men are hardly groundless: reported HIV/AIDS diagnoses in men who have sex with men, which had declined annually on average from 2001 to 2003 in a majority of American states, rose more than 3 percent in 2004, followed by a 6 percent jump in 2005 and another increase of nearly 4 percent in 2006—all in all, a sharp rise of 13.3 percent over the course of three years from 2003 to 2006 (though it is not clear how much of that rise should be put down to increased HIV testing or the duplication of diagnoses; moreover, the estimated number of newly diagnosed cases of AIDS among gay and bisexual men in the entire United States did not significantly increase from 2002 to 2006, the last year for which the CDC has provided comprehensive data).[27] In any case, the alarm over barebacking is certainly motivated by some quite real and ominous developments, but it may turn out to have been overblown—or, even, in some instances, to be mistaken.

For one thing, initial reports of barebacking often referred to condomless sex among men who had *already* been infected with HIV. All subsequent research has consistently shown that barebacking is practiced more frequently by men who are HIV-positive than by men who are HIV-negative. Furthermore, those HIV-positive men who bareback do it most often with men who either are or are assumed to be HIV-positive, or who are assumed to know that their partner is or is likely to be HIV-positive (very few HIV-positive men are willing to bareback with men they know to be HIV-negative).[28] Medical authorities have cautioned against unprotected anal sex between HIV-positive partners, fearing the possibility of "superinfection," the reinfection of an already infected person with a different and possibly more virulent or drug-resistant strain of HIV; accordingly, safe sex campaigns in the United States and Europe have often urged HIV-positive men to use condoms in anal sex with one another. But no hard evidence has so far materialized to justify that conservative prevention message: the authors of a recent literature review conclude that "the true rates and consequences of HIV superinfection have yet to be well delineated," and they point out that superinfection, though it can occur and has been documented, especially among newly infected individuals (at annual incidence rates as high as 5 percent) and among individuals who have interrupted treatment, is not well attested in the scientific literature (only sixteen cases reported worldwide between 2002 and 2005). In fact, exposure to different strains of HIV-1 regularly fails to produce expected occurrences of superinfection.[29] To the

extent that it takes place among HIV-positive partners—
or among HIV-negative partners, for that matter—barebacking carries no established risk of transmitting HIV
and so provides no immediate cause for alarm on that
score.

Indeed, the conscious and deliberate practice of
confining unprotected sex to relations between seroconcordant gay men (gay men who have the same HIV-
serostatus), a practice that is coming to be favored by gay
men in cities where the numbers of HIV-positive individuals allow for sufficient latitude and ease in the selection of
sexual partners, is now being hailed as a new "safe sex"
technique called "serosorting." For example, serosorting
has recently been credited with sharply reducing the rate of
HIV transmission among gay men in San Francisco since
2001 (though the claimed decline in the transmission rate
may misrepresent the available data, and the ascription of
that supposed decline to serosorting is a matter of interpretation).[30] And on November 6, 2006, the Department
of Public Health in San Francisco unveiled a new social
marketing campaign to promote serosorting as a means of
HIV/AIDS prevention. Called "Disclosure" and produced
by Better World Advertising, the campaign consists of bus
shelter and billboard posters that feature the message,
"Disclosure is HIV prevention," explaining that "Status
sorting is a prevention strategy" and urging gay men to
"test & tell."[31]

As Kane Race (a sociologist and HIV/AIDS researcher
who is one of the most astute commentators on the epidemic and its impact on gay men's sexual culture) has
pointed out, much of what was vilified as "barebacking" in
the mid-1990s, and is often denounced today as evidence
of gay men's pathological self-destructiveness, is in fact
precisely what is now being celebrated under the revamped
designation of "serosorting." The different valences
attached to the two terms do not necessarily result from
any difference in the nature of the sexual behaviors to
which they refer. After all, as Race observes, in many cases

barebacking and *serosorting* are simply alternate names for the same practice. The two words differ less in what they describe than in their respective interpretations of what condomless sex is all about. If "barebacking" alarmingly presents unprotected sex as a sign of irresponsible, hedonistic, reckless abandon on the part of gay men, Race argues, that is because it ignores the sexual protocols being worked out within HIV-positive communities and treats the rejection of condoms as an expression of unconstrained, libertine individualism. "Serosorting," by contrast, reassuringly implies a set of communal, hygienic arrangements for containing the virus within stable relationships, and it generates an image that foregrounds not the pleasure-seeking individual but the prudent, conjugal couple.[32]

Serosorting can reduce the risk of HIV transmission for individuals, but it certainly does not eliminate it, and it may even introduce new risks. For example, many young men in the United States who have been infected with HIV wrongly believe themselves to be HIV-negative. When the practice of serosorting leads men who actually *are* HIV-negative to have condomless sex with men who sincerely but mistakenly *believe* they are HIV-negative, such HIV-negative men put themselves at a very significant risk of infection with HIV.[33] In which case serosorting turns out to be a snare and a delusion. Also, HIV-negative men may not always have the insider knowledge of HIV-positive gay men's sexual culture that they require in order to pick up the tacit, subtle hints that HIV-positive men may think they are clearly dropping about their HIV-positive status.[34] And both HIV-negative and HIV-positive men may overestimate the degree to which their partners can correctly infer their true serostatus from the kinds of sexual behaviors they engage in or the sorts of risks they are willing to take.[35] The new emphasis on disclosure as a prevention strategy, as Kane Race points out, may even backfire, insofar as it could give HIV-negative men the false impression that HIV-positive men routinely

announce their serostatus and that those who don't identify themselves unambiguously as HIV-positive are not
infected.[36] Much serosorting, especially among young,
HIV-negative men, has therefore been redescribed as
"seroguessing."[37] So the efficacy of serosorting as a safe-sex
technique is not assured: it varies in accordance with frequency of HIV testing, accuracy of knowledge of one's
serostatus, explicitness of disclosure among sexual partners, and the sheer amount of HIV present within a particular network or population of individuals who have sex
with one another. And the only kind of serosorting that is
sure to be safe as a prevention technique is the serosorting
practiced among self-identified HIV-positive men, since
they are the ones who are most likely to know what their
true serostatus is (and someone who tells you he is positive
is probably not lying to you).

Nonetheless, to the extent that "barebacking" may turn
out to coincide, or at least to overlap, with "serosorting,"
it may not represent quite such an alarming development,
especially in sexual cultures in which gay men are well
informed about their true serostatus and are willing (or
empowered) to disclose it. By contrast, barebacking that
involves *deliberate, intentional unprotected sex between
HIV-positive and HIV-negative men,* though it may be fan-
tasized about, practiced, or even celebrated among a few
fringe groups,[38] seems to be extremely rare. Race notes that
"the only quantitative study to strictly define and describe
barebacking so far found that 229 (91%) of the 252 HIV-
negative and untested men surveyed who had heard of the
term *barebacking* had *not* 'intentionally set out to have
unprotected anal sex with someone other than a primary
partner' in the previous 2 years."[39] And the broadest statistical and demographic measures confirm that nearly 90
percent of all HIV-negative men who have sex with men in
the United States continue to avoid unprotected anal sex
with potentially HIV-positive men.[40] This generalization
holds even for men advertising for condomless sex on special Internet sites catering to barebackers: contrary to what

the mass media would often lead us to believe, the vast majority of men who use such websites to meet sexual partners for unprotected anal intercourse do *not* set out to be infected with HIV, or to infect others, but rather use serosorting or other techniques to minimize the risk of HIV transmission.[41] There is ample reason, in short, for reining in some of the recent panic about the supposed outbreak of unrestrained, irrational, and self-destructive risk-taking on the part of gay men.

❧ *In this context,* it is important to recall that "safe sex" (a set of practical guidelines for sexual behavior designed to reduce or eliminate the transmission of HIV), which remains the best hope for stopping the epidemic,[42] was originally a gay, grassroots invention. It was created by gay communities in North America and propagated throughout them even before an infectious agent associated with AIDS was discovered; it has continued to undergo periodic renovation ever since, as gay men informally but collectively revise their procedures for protecting themselves and their partners from infection in the light of changing medical technologies, increased experience of them, and more sophisticated mutual understanding.[43] Safe sex has proven to be overwhelmingly effective in preventing HIV transmission and reducing the prevalence of HIV infection in many parts of the world.[44] Already by the end of the 1980s, epidemiologists noted that documented changes in gay men's sexual behavior constituted "the most profound modifications of personal health-related behaviors ever recorded."[45] Recently, the authors of an authoritative epidemiological report on sexual practices in Australia observed, "In general, the majority of homosexually active men have sustained a 'safe sex' culture [since the advent of the HIV/AIDS epidemic] even though sustaining safe sex over such a long period is difficult."[46] That poker-faced final clause is a masterpiece of understatement.

In the United States alone, white gay men—once the main vector of HIV transmission—now account for less than a quarter of new HIV infections.[47] In fact, barely more than a third of the *entire* new AIDS caseload reported in 2006 (the latest year for which statistics are available in the United States at the time I am writing) can be traced specifically to gay sex.[48] Summing up the data for Europe, Canada, Australia, and the United States, one researcher has recently noted that, despite the evidence of an increase in sexual risk-taking, "the majority of gay men continued to report safer sex practice" in the period since the introduction of the new generation of antiretroviral therapies in 1996. And a number of recent studies indicate that sexual risk-taking by gay men may now be leveling off or even declining.[49]

Serosorting represents merely the latest chapter in this ongoing saga. Indeed, as Kane Race has lately reminded us, the evolution of safe sex practices indicates that "risk" and "safety" are not opposites or alternatives. Much of what now qualifies as "safe sex" is the result of gay men's spontaneous improvisations, their calculated experimentation with varying degrees of risk. After all, the medical establishment in the United States never told us it was safe to have sex, let alone that sex was good for us. They still have not given us a green light to practice unprotected oral sex (even without ejaculation).[50] Nor did they say we could have as many sexual partners as we wanted so long as what we did with them was safe. They have never endorsed condomless sex among HIV-positive men or agreements among HIV-negative partners in a stable relationship to have unprotected sex with each other so long as they protect themselves from infection in their contacts with casual sexual partners: this technique, a precursor of serosorting, was identified in 1991–92 by Susan Kippax and her team of Australian social researchers into gay men's sexual practices and included by them in their new category of "negotiated safety," but that practice has not been consistently promoted as a prevention technique by public health authorities in the United States.[51] The American medical establishment never even told us it was safe to kiss.

It is gay men themselves who have continued to define, and to redefine, the limits of safety through an ongoing history of sexual experimentation and mutual consultation, and who have thereby produced, over time, workable compromises and pragmatic solutions that balance safety and risk in proportions that have turned out to be both acceptable to a majority of gay men and successful in limiting the transmission of HIV.[52] The upturn in condomless sex that we have been witnessing recently does not signal the end of safe sex, the failure of HIV prevention, or a new indifference on the part of gay men to the risks of HIV infection (after all, as Michael Shernoff points out, there have always been some gay men who, for whatever reason, have preferred to take significant risks in their sexual practices).[53] The current loosening of the condom code may simply be the latest stage in the ongoing evolution of harm reduction techniques among men who have sex with men, the most recent adjustment or refinement in the complex protocols of safe sex.

Some of the probabilistic calculations behind this loosening of safe sex practices may be merely wishful or careless, even misguided and dangerous, so there is good reason to be concerned about the possibility that the growing experimentation with condomless sex may lead to increased transmission of HIV, especially among the young, the poor, the badly served and badly informed, or those who do not consider themselves gay. We should certainly remain alert to the way that harm reduction techniques, even among relatively canny and self-aware gay men, can sometimes lead to new possibilities for harm *increase*.[54] But there do not seem to be grounds for believing that gay men as a whole have suddenly abandoned the cause of HIV prevention or given up on either the idea or the practice of safe sex. The evidence hardly supports the generalization, currently being popularized by psychoanalytic theorist Tim Dean, that "erotic risk among gay men has become organized and deliberate, not just accidental."[55]

On the contrary. Although there does appear to have been an increase in condomless sex among men who have sex with men, it does not follow that there has been an increase in *deliberate* risk-taking. Some of the new harm reduction techniques that have been substituted for the use of condoms may not be as effective as they are intended to be, but the data do not require us to conclude that gay men have massively renounced safe sex as a goal in favor of what Dean calls "purposeful HIV-transmission."[56] Rather, what we may be witnessing is a change in the definition and concrete manifestations of safe sex, which have moved HIV prevention practices beyond the antiquated, unworkable rule of "use a condom every time." While there are new risks associated with this trend—risks that are hardly trivial, as the recent rise in reported HIV/AIDS diagnoses in American men who have sex with men suggests, and that therefore demand to be addressed—there is little reason to presume that gay men no longer consider HIV/AIDS prevention an urgent matter, that they have accepted new levels of risk as a matter of course, or that their behavior reveals the symptoms of a collective psychological affliction.[57]

"How do we measure the success or failure of HIV prevention?" Eric Rofes asked in 1998.

If we use what appears to be the common standard driving most HIV-education programs, we view each new infection of a gay man as evidence of failure and proclaim there is an expansion of the epidemic. While literally true in aggregate numbers of infected gay men, this kind of evaluation is inappropriate for use with communicable diseases that require long-term, sustained approaches and achievable goals. To mistake the utopian rhetoric that we could end AIDS tomorrow if everyone practiced safe sex 100 percent of the time for appropriate public health strategy is terribly misguided. Instead, I believe the way to assess our prevention efforts is by examining the level of seroprevalence within successive generations of gay men. A realistic aim might be that each successive cohort of gay men in a particular location show a specific decline in level of infection. . . . Rather than a crisis-driven, drama-queen exaggeration of continuing HIV infection among gay men, coming to terms with the AIDS epidemic means confronting the authentic reality we face. . . .[58]

The spread of epidemic disease is notoriously difficult to stop by means of behavioral interventions alone. And yet nearly two-thirds of gay men in the United States contrive to remain uninfected over the long term.[59]

Gay men have rarely gotten credit for those lifesaving breakthroughs, however, either in scientific or in popular writing about the epidemic. Nimmons discovered that "a literature search on 'gay men, HIV, and risk factors' finds some 588 studies, yet the same search on 'gay men, HIV and safety' yields only nine. Of those, only eight papers explicitly set out to chronicle the native strategies gay men have developed, the affirmative and creative ways ordinary people have invented to protect each other."[60] Gay men are more likely to see the continued existence of male-to-male HIV transmission (at annual rates ranging from a stubborn and unacceptably high 1 percent to a truly terrifying 4 percent or more among some younger men and some African American men) used against them, while their scattered departures from perfect adherence to safe-sex protocols typically occasion global judgments about their impaired or abnormal psychology.[61] Only 61 percent of Americans in 1996 consistently reported using seatbelts, according to the National Highway Traffic Safety Administration, as Nimmons pointed out, but that statistic—which, thankfully, has since improved—did not raise comparably grave concerns about the mental health of the heterosexual majority. Similarly, the most recent literature review analyzing the causes of risky sexual behavior among young heterosexual women and men looked exclusively to social factors for explanation, never to psychological ones.[62]

The alleged failure of safe sex campaigns and the defective psychology of gay men that has been posited to explain it are quickly laid at the door of all gay men without qualification. Particular blame has lately been attached to those non-white gay and bisexual men in the United States among whom HIV/AIDS diagnoses have recently been increasing at the sharpest rates in the nation—even though a careful study of a multiethnic population of gay men in San Francisco determined that "the prevalence of bare-backing did not differ by race/ethnicity."[63] In particular, the higher rate of infection among black men who have sex with men does not correlate with higher levels of docu-mented risk-taking. As one researcher sums up the current findings, "Black men who have sex with men (BMSM) are disproportionately affected by HIV/AIDS in the United States. . . . Yet the disparity is not explained by higher rates of unprotected anal and oral sex."[64] This crux in the avail-able data makes it particularly hazardous to generalize about the relation between race and risk in black commu-nities, to say nothing of assigning blame. Nonetheless, epi-demiological evidence provides a convenient vehicle for ratifying moral and psychological judgments against those who are already devalued on the grounds of sexuality or race (or both); members of socially privileged groups, by contrast, suffer only individual, not collective, discredita-tion. HIV/AIDS prevention allows such a normalizing strategy to proceed under the protective, politically virtu-ous cover of enlightened concern for the downtrodden, and stigmatized groups are pathologized on the pretext of victim advocacy.

❧ *In order to* explain why some small proportion of gay men continue to take certain risks in their sexual practices, even in the third decade of the HIV/AIDS epidemic, both scientists and journalists have to reckon with gay men's motivations for risk-taking, which means in turn that they have to address the topic of gay sexual subjectivity, what gay men want. HIV/AIDS prevention has now come to be the one genre of public discourse in which gay male subjectivity, far from being bracketed or sidelined, is a continual subject of discussion. The focus on gay subjectivity is sharpest in the case of white, socially privileged gay men, whose agency and autonomy are not likely to have been compromised by political oppression or external constraint and whose behavior therefore cannot be explained by other social factors: that is why much of what I have to say here will refer to them, though my conclusions will have a wider application.[65]

Most often the efforts to account for gay men's risk-taking, as Gregory Tomso notes, revolve obsessively around a single, rather unhelpful question—"What makes them do it?"—which then leads directly to an entire series of unwarranted and even crude (if sometimes well-meaning) psychological speculations about the nature of gay male subjectivity itself.[66] What is it that goes on in the minds and hearts and psyches of gay men? What makes them tick? What makes them so different from normal people? Why do they behave so badly, so irrationally, so self-destructively? What is wrong with them? What determines the affective structure of their feelings and impulses? Why do they seem to be so impervious to HIV/AIDS prevention efforts? And what picture can we draw, on that basis, of the peculiar and characteristic features of gay male subjectivity itself?

It is probably pointless to try and explain why anyone has unprotected sex. There are obvious contributing factors to the practice of risk, which it is always useful to analyze,[67] but plumbing the depths of human motivation in search of ultimate causes is a bad idea, because it is likely to produce specious answers. The notion that people, once they truly understand what is in their own best interests, always act rationally in order to maximize them—on the basis of an accurate, long-term calculation of the likely costs and benefits of their behavior—has taken a persistent battering ever since Socrates first proposed it. Rational calculation does not always explain even the sort of human behavior most amenable to cost-benefit analysis, namely economic behavior. (Just think of global warming.) Human beings tend to have a hard time giving up something they badly want, when it is ready to hand, for the sake of a less immediate and more long-term benefit. Why should we suppose that sex, of all things, would be the sphere in which people could be depended on to act in a *more* rational or calculating fashion than they typically do?

Especially since sex without condoms is fun.

As Stephen Lyng and his colleagues have shown, modern Westerners have a very complicated relation to risk that can, however, be summed up pretty quickly. Risk is thrilling.[68] It hardly seems surprising that sexual behavior, whose thrills are routinely intensified by various sorts of risk (pregnancy, infidelity, naughtiness, pain, shame, disgust, disease, love), does not readily lend itself to consistent and careful calculation or control.[69]

In fact, what seems truly remarkable is not that some people continue to take some risks in their sexual practices, but that such a large proportion of gay men should have succeeded for so long in adhering so prudently to so many constraining and annoying limitations on their sexual behavior. To speculate about the peculiar subjectivity of gay men on the basis of their occasional sexual risk-taking is a misguided project. There is, in all likelihood, nothing in particular to explain beyond the obvious: sex is easier and more pleasurable without condoms, and people have a hard time consistently and categorically foregoing a pleasure they deeply cherish when they have to do it over a very long period of time. It was never realistic to expect that HIV/AIDS alone would "provide the requisite motivation for sweeping behavior changes" or that it would lead people to jettison *en masse* and without a backward glance the sexual activities central to their senses of themselves.[70]

The narrator of a forthcoming novel/memoir by Kirk Read puts it very well:

I grew up post-AIDS, where I wasn't privy to some collective generational memory of what it was like before the epidemic.

I knew it felt better. I mean, that's the dirty little secret of bareback sex, the thing nobody ever says out loud. It feels better. *You feel more connected to the person you're with, the friction is smoother, there's a sort of abandon that's intoxicating. The Centers for Disease Control never includes that basic, obvious truth in press releases:* It feels better.

You know what I'm talking about, where they take a street survey that isn't even remotely scientific—like 250 gay men in one neighborhood of one city randomly selected by young non-profit wage slaves with a clipboard questionnaire. Then they turn it into a huge pronouncement that unprotected anal sex is on the rise by 48% in urban gay men and it's all because gay men have low self-esteem. And all these medical "experts" line up to shake their fingers, especially at the young ones who should know better, those of us who didn't lose all of our friends in the 80s. They say we're suicidal. They never just say We're really sorry. Condoms suck. We know it feels better. We just have to do this for a while. *Why can't the government say that? Even a lot of HIV positive guys are self-righteous, saying they have no sympathy for anyone who gets infected in this day and age, knowing what we know. Like they had no idea it could happen to them. Like they were all infected in 1978, back before we all got kicked out of Eden. Honey, no one's innocent and everyone's innocent. It's complicated. It's context.*[71]

Although not all research into gay men's sexual practices is as inept as the kind of behavioral survey that Read's narrator lampoons, he is right to protest about the way alarmist statistics are used to generate punitive judgments about the sanity of gay men. He is also right to believe that the question of why some gay men have risky sex is itself badly formulated and prejudicial.

I find it unfortunate to have to enter a discussion of gay male subjectivity that has already been framed by the question of why some gay men have risky sex, a discussion that cannot fail to lend the question itself a substance and a dignity it has no right to claim. One of the purposes of this essay is to argue that the very question "What makes them do it?" produces, inevitably and necessarily, bad and irrelevant answers. Far from opening up new perspectives on sex and risk, it simply creates the unfortunate presumption that there is something wrong with particular groups and individuals. In order to confront sexual risk-taking both practically and imaginatively, we need to take it out of the realm of morality and normalizing judgments (whatever our personal feelings about it may be). And instead of representing sexual risk in the era of AIDS as a vertiginous high-wire act, a drama of virtue forever teetering on the brink of the abyss, we might begin by trying to de-dramatize the practice of risk-taking altogether.[72]

That is precisely what Lauren Berlant proposes to do in a highly original essay on obesity, to which I shall have occasion to refer a number of times in what follows. Her analysis of everyday practices and habits "focuses on what's vague and gestural about the subject and episodic about the event. It presumes nothing about the meaning of decision or the impact of an act." Berlant argues that unless we attend "to the varieties of constraint and unconsciousness that condition ordinary activity," we are likely to ascribe an excess of meaning to particular acts, to endow modern subjects with an untrammeled sovereignty, an inflated capacity of cognition, and a powerful, effective, consequential agency that they do not in fact possess, and to ascribe to them on that erroneous basis a heightened responsibility such that all their actions take on the melodramatic intensity of a life-or-death decision. She prefers, instead,

to rethink some taxonomies of causality, subjectivity, and life making embedded in normative notions of agency. More particularly, I want to suggest that to continue to counter the moral science of biopolitics, which links the political administration of life to a melodrama of the care of the monadic self, we need to think about agency and personhood not only in normative terms but also as activity exercised within spaces of

*ordinariness that does not always or even usually follow the lit-
eralizing logic of visible effectuality, bourgeois dramatics, and
lifelong accumulation or fashioning. . . . I recast these within
a zone of temporality we can gesture toward as that of ongoingness, getting by, and living on, where the structural
inequalities are dispersed, the pacing of their experience inter-
mittent, often in phenomena not prone to capture by a consciousness organized by archives of memorable impact. I want
to prompt a thought about a kind of interruptive agency that
aspires to detach from a condition or to diminish being meaningful. Crisis management produces dramas that obscure the
motives and temporalities of these aspects of living.*[73]

Despite the somewhat enigmatic language in which it is
couched, Berlant's project is an admirable one. Its importance lies in its attempt to move us beyond the familiar
binary model that positions the hypercognitive, well-disci-
plined, rational, and calculating neoliberal subject over
against his shadowy opposite, the pathological, defective,
victimized, reason-impaired subject. That is precisely the
set of false alternatives that we need to get past if we are to
rethink sex and risk productively in the context of
HIV/AIDS prevention.

The only problem with Berlant's approach for the purpose of de-dramatizing the practice of sexual risk is that her
model of "ongoingness" does not lend itself to the phenomenology of HIV infection. There is nothing "episodic"
about the event of HIV transmission: it happens once, and
it may even happen suddenly, in a transient instant. HIV
infection does not occur according to the slow temporalities of obesity; on the contrary, nothing could be more calculated to restore to "the event" its singularity and narrative prestige. Sexual risk and HIV transmission would
seem to have a kind of melodrama built into them.
Although the degree of risk involved in any one act of
unprotected sex between an infected and an uninfected
partner is very slight, a single, momentary contact *can* have
life-changing consequences. The stark realities of sexual

risk may tend, if anything, to intensify the melodramatics of responsibility, intentionality, agency, and moral seriousness that already attach to the scene of gay male sex in the context of the HIV/AIDS epidemic and that complicate the work of prevention.

Nonetheless, if there is nothing episodic about HIV transmission, there may well be much that is episodic about condomless sex. So that is where the usefulness of Berlant's approach may lie. In actual practice, sexual risk may partake of precisely the sort of intermittence, ongoingness, and ordinariness that Berlant evokes. That is true especially to the extent that condomless sex can become, within the context of an individual life, a cumulative habit without a specific accompanying consciousness, an unreflective tendency, a gradual or occasional letting-go of meaning, agency, will, or cognition.

In any case, it will be important to find some way to evade the choice between the rational subject and the pathological subject, as well as some way to take the drama out of the practice of risk. In order to do that, we may need to move HIV/AIDS away from the center of all thinking about gay men's sexual health. As the late Eric Rofes argued eloquently for more than a decade, the health of gay men ought to be conceptualized in an affirmative, holistic, politically imaginative fashion. It should not be narrowly defined by purely medical thinking about HIV/AIDS, reduced to the treatment of pathologies, or overwhelmed by panic scenarios about the epidemic.[74] For all of these reasons, it is crucial to detach our models of gay male subjectivity from discourses of mental health, the high moral drama of the individual sexual act, the dichotomous opposition between rational agency and pathology, and the epidemiology of risk.

But that is not what I am going to do here—at least, not right away. As I will contend, we cannot afford in the present context *not* to challenge the new, medicalized model of gay male subjectivity, even if challenging it means accepting, for the purposes of argument, the damaging premises on which it is based. It is with regret, then, but also with full consideration of the larger context, that I continue to focus here on the connections between sexual risk-taking and gay male subjectivity—even though maintaining those connections cannot advance the larger project of promoting gay men's health by freeing it from an obsessive concern with HIV transmission. If I still think it is worth taking up the question of why some gay men have risky sex, despite the regrettable ways the question itself may distract from more constructive approaches to gay men's sexual health, that is because I believe it is important to respond to the revival of psychopathological thinking about gay male subjectivity that the topic of risky sex has unfortunately inspired.

Whether we like it or not, the perennial need for effective HIV/AIDS prevention strategies has once again made it possible, as well as politically palatable, to ask in all seriousness a battery of psychological and psychoanalytic questions about the nature of gay male subjectivity that had long been considered quaint, pointless, or prejudicial, and that had in any case been discredited by their implication in the protracted and shameful history of pseudoscientific homophobia. It is as if the very indecorousness of the topic of unprotected anal intercourse, coupled with the undoubted epidemiological imperative to address its occurrence among gay men, has emboldened researchers to break the various taboos that, in progressive circles at least, had previously prohibited any substantive discussion of the subjective life of male homosexuality.

Whatever the explanation, the fact remains that learned and journalistic discourses about why some gay men take chances in their sexual practices have led to the construction of *new subjectivities of risk* as well as to the creation of new public venues in which it is now possible to ask, with a straight face, "What do gay men want?" If only for that reason, it is important to challenge those discourses—even though, by assuming the unnecessary burden of explaining why some gay men have risky sex, the challenge itself has to be conducted on terms already inimical to the interests of gay men. Indeed, the unwelcome answers to the question of what gay men want that have already been provided by many HIV/AIDS researchers reveal a lot about why the lesbian and gay movement tried to bracket that question in the first place—and they thereby increase the pressure on us to find other ways of asking and answering it.

❧ *It is of course* legitimate to guard against increases in sexual risk-taking by gay men. To the extent that such increases are accurately documented, they should arouse real concern and evoke a vigorous and sustained response. The minority of gay men who put themselves at significant risk of HIV infection deserve a disproportionate amount of attention from epidemiologists and prevention activists, since those gay men are the ones whose behavior presents a challenge to public health and threatens to enlarge the scope of the epidemic both within gay communities and beyond them. It is therefore understandable that so much interest should be devoted to the percentage of gay men who fail to protect themselves adequately from the danger of HIV infection, nor is there anything particularly sinister about the fact of such interest in itself. The current panic over the alleged failure of safe-sex education, however, goes beyond the scope of the actual problem and produces a number of unfortunate results.

First, it exaggerates the extent of the danger (which is real but not desperate). Next, it intensifies the obsession with risky sex, making it seem central to the definition of gay male identity in the present—and therefore harder to resist. The sensationalistic treatment of gay male risk-takers portrays gay men themselves as the sole source of the problem, as if they were to blame for the absence in the United States of any public support for a vibrant, sophisticated, and safe gay sexual culture as well as for the lack of publicly available, explicit, precise, reliable, appropriate, and practical information about how to prevent HIV infection. It substitutes for these social and political factors a multitude of moral and psychological ones, and it treats as inexplicable lapses gay men's principled refusals to adhere unswervingly to outdated, unrealistic, or excessively stringent safe-sex protocols. The moral and psychological defects from which gay male risk-takers supposedly suffer are then generalized, categorically extended to lesbians, bisexuals, and gay men as a group. In this way, public discourses about "the return of unsafe sex" have contributed to the repathologizing of homosexuality. And so they affect queer people as a whole.

The tendency to approach the problem of HIV/AIDS prevention by asking what is wrong with individual gay men who take sexual risks—an approach that, historically, has been characteristic of the United States—probably dates back to the late 1980s. In the latter part of that decade, according to Nicolas Sheon and G. Michael Crosby, the rise of HIV-antibody testing split the gay world into two populations ("HIV-positive and HIV-unknown"), and that split led in turn to a "shift . . . away from community-centered discussions of norms to an emphasis on individual risk calculus and decision-making." The transformation was also reflected, they contend, by a change in "the focus of prevention interventions which became increasingly centered around individualized risk assessment and education. . . . Essentially, the HIV antibody test initiated a shift away from communal, existential questions like 'why do *we* do what we do' to [the] individual-focused, epistemological question of 'how do *you* know what you know?'"[75] Prevention ceased in this way to be a matter of collective, communal responsibility and became a matter of duty (or its dereliction) on the part of individuals. And as gay communities tended to break up, disperse, and become more diversified as a result of the many deaths from AIDS, the skyrocketing property values in American cities that followed a wave of gentrification in the same period, and the arrival of new, younger urban migrants, gay male life became more segmented and atomistic, and community norms lost their power to shape individual behavior.[76] The management of sexual risk in the United States thus became increasingly individualized.

It is in this context that the gay male subject of unsafe sex, as Barry Adam maintains, has come to represent the cultural antithesis of the "calculating, rational, self-interested subject" who now constitutes the presumptive subject of free-market neoliberalism and, thus, the new model of the "autonomous, self-regulated individual" in our disciplinary societies—the notional norm of a responsible, self-governing Everyman.[77] It is at least partly because the gay male subject of unsafe sex represents such a scandalous rebuke to neoliberal models of individual rationality that, in the last dozen years or so, a vast scientific and popular literature has come into being that focuses with a kind of horrified fascination on the minority of gay men who have risky sex.

One effect of that literature has been to produce a new and exotic bestiary of barebackers, bug chasers, gift givers, and other adepts of extreme sensation, whose behavior is explained by reference to their intellectual or emotional "deficits." Such deficits include the "preset psychological variables" of "low self-esteem, sexual identity problems, or general sexual impulsivity," which are then compounded by "a host of irrational intervening factors: complacent AIDS optimists, reason-impaired drug users, personality-defective sensation seekers, and so on," culminating in "the panic icons of the popular imagination: demon infectors . . . , monster AIDS transmitters" as well as "barebackers and their mirror image, bug chasers, nearly always reported third hand or as seen on the internet."[78] (It is the researchers and writers who pursue these creatures, more than gay men themselves, who deserve to be labeled "bug chasers," as Michele Morales has pointed out.)[79]

Gregory Tomso, who has also studied the various discourses surrounding this topic, observes that "the list of reasons" given in the recent literature for gay men's engaging in risky sexual behavior is "expansive: low self-esteem; the physical pleasures of condomless sex; a 'culture of dis-

ease' created by glossy HIV-medication ads that equate
infection with 'popularity and acceptance'; childhood sexual abuse; drug use; rebellion against authority; 'sexual
self-control deficits'; and the eroticization of risk itself, to
name just a few."[80]

In short, just when sexual difference was finally getting
distinguished from pathology, just when homosexuality
was ceasing to be considered a sickness, just when
HIV/AIDS was at last starting to be recognized as a global
pandemic, a public health emergency, and a terrible historical accident instead of being portrayed as a gothic tale
of sexual crime and punishment—just at that moment a
new syndrome, that of the psychologically afflicted gay
individual who knowingly seeks to be infected or to infect
others with HIV, has restored to homosexuality its venera-
ble identity as a disease.[81]

❧ *Out of the* vast and repellent literature on the supposed
irrationality and self-destructiveness of gay men who take
risks in their sexual practices, I will present just one trivial
if typical example. I have chosen it not for its outlandish
rhetoric or sexual demonology—the prize for that could
probably go to the notorious 2003 *Rolling Stone* feature,
"In Search of Death"[82]—but, on the contrary, for its
banality and relative inoffensiveness (though I would
hardly want to minimize its power to offend). On September 24, 2002, the *New York Times* published an article by
Dr. Richard A. Friedman entitled, "A Clue to Why Gays
Play Russian Roulette With H.I.V." The occasion for that
typically sensationalistic representation of gay men's relation to risk turns out to have been a study presented at the
14th International Conference on HIV/AIDS in
Barcelona, which found that 77 percent of a group of
fifteen- to twenty-nine-year-old HIV-positive "gay and
bisexual" men were unaware that they had been infected
with HIV, despite supposedly having engaged in sexual
behavior that might have exposed them to the virus. The

authors of the study freely admitted that their figure of 77 percent was "upwardly biased to some unknown extent," but you would never know that from reading the article in the *New York Times,* which presented that excessively high figure at face value without further qualification—and as if the prevalence of unrecognized HIV infection did not vary wildly from one country to another, clearly correlating with differences in local social and political conditions (which should warn us not to seek its causes in individual gay men's psychology).[83] Undeterred by such considerations, Dr. Friedman went on to ask, "How can one explain such potentially fatal self-destructive behavior? . . . Why would anyone knowingly expose himself to a potentially lethal infection?"

In response to his own questions, with their gratuitous ascriptions to queer men of extreme self-destructiveness and conscious death-seeking, Dr. Friedman appealed to the work of Columbia psychiatrist Richard C. Friedman (no relation). The latter, identified as the coauthor of a promising new book entitled *Sexual Orientation and Psychoanalysis,*[84] located one cause of "this dangerous behavior" in "a phenomenon called internalized homophobia." That phenomenon is characterized by both Drs. Friedman as "a common and often serious psychological problem in gay men and women that lies at the root of many self-destructive behaviors, including risky sex." Note that the explanation for the irrational behavior of the risk-taking subgroup of gay men is generalized here and immediately made to apply to "gay men *and women*" without qualification, who are then described as being given to "*many* (other, unspecified) self-destructive behaviors, including"—but by no means limited to—"risky sex."

What is enlightening about this article is obviously not the insight it purports to offer into what it called "an aspect" of gay male sexual life "that has eluded explanation" until now. After all, "internalized homophobia" hasn't been news for at least thirty years, and the invocation of that notion here merely provides a politically palatable cover for the continued, insistent association of queer people with psychopathology. (Would the *New York Times* ascribe "serious psychological problems" to heterosexual women as a class and diagnose them all as suffering from "internalized misogyny" because some of them sometimes "play Russian roulette" with pregnancy? It's an intriguing idea, in its way, even if it is misguided for the reasons I have already mentioned, but in any case we shouldn't expect to see it expressed very soon in the *New York Times*.) As lesbian psychologist Celia Kitzinger argued twenty years ago, "internalized homophobia" is the gay-affirmative version of homosexual pathology: it is not their homosexuality but their homophobia that now makes queer people sick.[85]

More recently, Peter Hegarty has established that nearly one-quarter of current research into homophobia by professional psychologists focuses not on straight people's aversion to queers but on queers' own supposed aversion to themselves. "In the last five years examined," he wrote in 2006, "24 per cent of the articles that mentioned homophobia concerned the ways that gay men, lesbians and bisexuals (in that order) internalised prejudice rather than the ways that heterosexuals endorsed or enacted it."[86] As Hegarty noted, summarizing a number of recent studies, internalized homophobia has become a favorite explanation among psychologists for why gay men have condomless anal sex, even though at least one literature review concluded that "the evidence for a link between unsafe sex among bisexual and gay men and internalised homophobia was weak at best."[87]

What the *New York Times* article does show is that the topic of "unsafe sex" opens up an inviting public space for respectable if misguided speculation about what gay men want, about the subjective life of male homosexuality. The article also dramatizes the urgent need for a counter-discourse of gay male subjectivity: not a wholesale avoidance of the subject, and not a more gay-friendly brand of psychology attentive to the disabling effects of homophobia—that, as the article itself illustrates, is already part of the problem—but a discourse free from psychology itself and from psychology's tainted opposition between the normal and the pathological.[88]

III

That is precisely what Michael Warner, a prominent queer theorist, attempted to provide in an eloquent, ambitious, and now largely forgotten article in a January 1995 issue of the *Village Voice* called "Unsafe: Why Gay Men Are Having Risky Sex."[89] Warner, along with Mark Shoofs (who for years covered HIV/AIDS issues for the *Voice*), felt impelled to speak out in order to sound an alarm about what looked to be a potentially dangerous breakdown in safer-sex practices among even well-informed and politically aware gay men in New York. Warner wanted to restart a conversation in the gay male community about HIV prevention. He was particularly concerned about attitudes to risk on the part of HIV-negative gay men, whose subjective lives had tended to be overshadowed, for good reason, by the urgent emotional and material needs of people living with HIV/AIDS. Warner made a striking effort to lay out some possibilities for how to think about gay men's relations to sex and risk, and he put questions of gay male subjectivity at the front and center of his analysis.

Even though Warner's article is dated in some crucial respects—it was written, after all, before highly active antiretroviral therapy had transformed HIV/AIDS from an acute, and fatal, disease into a chronic and largely manageable one—it remains important for my purposes. It was an early attempt to think about gay men's risk-taking without recourse to psychology, and it demonstrates the advantages of such a non-psychologizing approach to sex and risk. Although Warner himself did not fully realize all those advantages in the article as it was published, the aim he sought to achieve remains, if anything, even more important and relevant now than it was in 1995.

The text of Warner's article is no longer readily accessible. I have therefore decided to reprint it in an appendix to this volume. And I am going to spend some time describing, discussing, and commenting on it. It may seem strange to lavish so much attention on what is now an outdated piece of occasional writing—whose cue for passion has since been superseded by changing medical realities—and even more strange to perform a close rhetorical analysis of it. But I believe that both Warner's successes and his failures continue to be exemplary in their different ways. Warner offers us a model for how to think about sex (including risky sex) in a non-normalizing fashion, free from the moralizing and therapeutic clichés of much psychological speculation. His lapses testify to the difficulty of sustaining such an approach. And the dangers those lapses entail indicate just how perilous the project is and why it is so important to get it right.

Warner's article dramatizes the urgency of rescuing the category of gay subjectivity from the blackout imposed on it by gay identity politics. It also dramatizes, however, the potential pitfalls of submitting the gay subject to a renewed analysis. It thereby constitutes a powerful warning of the need to insist on finding alternatives to psychology and psychoanalysis if we are to reintroduce the category of gay subjectivity into the frame of a gay analysis—especially if we are to do so without risking a return of hoary pathological judgments about the subjective life of male homosexuality and without incurring all the liabilities that the punitive discourses surrounding gay men who have risky sex so abundantly and vividly illustrate.

❧ *In firing off* his essay to the *Voice*, Warner was reacting with some haste to the particular situation of urgent need in which gay men and gay male sexual culture found themselves during the early 1990s in the United States, with its perennial lack of an adequate national response to the HIV/AIDS emergency. "There has never been a national plan that comprehensively addresses HIV prevention, treatment, and other related needs within the country's borders—and there is no comprehensive strategic plan to address AIDS today," concluded an authoritative report published in 2006, twenty-five years into the known epidemic.[90] Given this continuing, calamitous failure of public resolve in the United States to deal systematically with the HIV/AIDS epidemic (which, admittedly, pales in comparison to the colossal failure to confront HIV/AIDS in Africa),[91] there is a constant need for new initiatives to halt the transmission of HIV. After all, estimated numbers of new HIV infections in the United States as a whole have not significantly declined in the past decade: from a low of about forty-nine thousand per year in the early 1990s, they rose to about fifty-eight thousand per year in the late 1990s before leveling off at about fifty-five thousand per year from 2000 to 2006, totaling approximately 56,300 in 2006 (the latest year for which the CDC has published estimates).[92]

In writing his article, then, Warner was trying to respond to this situation, and in particular to the need for new prevention strategies targeting men who have sex with men. Already by the winter of 1994–95, it was plain to Warner and many other observers that established guidelines for gay male sexual behavior that had been laid down ten years earlier in the United States, with the aim of stopping the transmission of HIV, were no longer up to the job of addressing the complex practical and ethical issues that gay men faced. For in that moment—that is, in the interval between the collapse of hope in the long-term therapeutic efficacy of AZT and the emergence of more effective antiretroviral therapies featuring different combinations of protease inhibitors—gay men were having to make what appeared at the time to be a definitive and permanent rearrangement of their sexual lives under the pressure of an unabating threat of lethal infection. Under those conditions, a prevention strategy designed to eliminate all risk of HIV transmission, which was and has remained to this very day the only official, widely endorsed prevention strategy in the United States, was bound to fail catastrophically.[93]

"How much risk is acceptable?" asked Warner. "For years the major prevention organizations—including GMHC [Gay Men's Health Crisis in New York City]—and government agencies said none. . . . By most accounts, a significant number of gay men—like most heterosexuals—have simply ignored the advice, or have set a goal of safer rather than absolutely safe sex" (33). After all, absolutely safe sex, as Warner quoted Walt Odets (a San Francisco therapist who has worked with HIV-negative gay men) as saying, means "never to touch another human being" (36).[94] And so it would seem that gay men were wise to reject a policy of *risk elimination* in favor of *risk reduction,* since risk elimination is virtually impossible to sustain over the long term, and twenty years is a very long time.

In fact, when it comes to sex, five minutes can be a long time.

Moreover, a strategy of risk elimination that is not sustainable is likely to result in highly risky periodic lapses, which makes it very dangerous. Whereas a strategy of risk reduction that is more workable is also likely to be more effective. And indeed it has proven to be successful in curtailing the HIV/AIDS epidemic among gay men in countries, such as Australia, where the policy of risk reduction has been a prominent feature of national HIV/AIDS prevention strategies from early on.[95]

In the United States, however, no such risk reduction strategy has ever been widely promoted.[96] Hence, Warner and other prevention activists had reason to be alarmed by emerging indications that as many as 30 to 60 percent of HIV-negative gay men in the United States, especially younger gay men, were having regular, unprotected anal intercourse with partners of unknown (or even positive)

HIV-serology status. Was this reported increase in unprotected anal intercourse among gay men to be understood as a dramatic increase in actual risk-taking? Or did it occur in the context of various countervailing practices of risk reduction, and, if so, how effective were those practices? In other words, did reports of an increased incidence of unprotected anal intercourse among gay men necessarily translate into evidence of a likely increase in HIV infection?

Given the lethal lack of detailed information in the United States about gay men's sexual practices, Warner unfortunately could not afford to linger over that crucial question. Instead, and not unreasonably at the time, Warner, along with many others, feared that "infection rates would explode" and unleash a "second wave" of the HIV/AIDS epidemic among gay men (33). This did not in fact occur, but it was sensible for Warner and others to worry about it at the time, given the alarming and imprecise nature of the information they possessed. Only by the end of the 1990s, in greatly changed circumstances, did transmission rates of HIV among gay and bisexual men stop declining and even begin to show signs of an increase in North America, Australia, and several major European cities, with a whopping 13.3 percent rise in reported name-based HIV/AIDS diagnoses due to male-to-male sexual contact in a majority of the United States from 2003 to 2006 (although the same period did not witness an overall increase in estimated cases of AIDS due to gay sex in the United States as a whole).[97]

In response to what seemed to be an alarming trend, Warner called for a radical reevaluation of U.S. education and prevention strategies addressed to gay men. As an essential first step towards that goal, he pleaded for "a better culture of discussion." He quoted one gay prevention activist as saying, "We haven't created the spaces where gay men can be honest with each other, and that's the beginning of harm reduction" (36). The dominant ethic of risk elimination, instead of risk reduction, in the United States made it impossible for gay men to admit openly to having unprotected anal intercourse without thereby branding themselves as criminals or traitors—without incurring the blame, shame, and guilt directed at them by other, less risk-tolerant (or less candid) gay men. So long as that was the case, it would obviously be impossible to confront sexual risk-taking in gay male communities, to forge new collective strategies of risk reduction, to adjust prevention initiatives to what seemed to have become a permanent state of medical crisis, or to produce a culture of practical sexual realism in the face of an ongoing threat of infection.

❧ *The most pressing* need in such a situation was an end to guilt-tripping prevention tactics that both failed to eliminate all risk-taking activities and inhibited an exploration of alternate prevention strategies by discouraging gay men from discussing frankly their sexual practices and the motives behind them—from addressing, that is, the topic of their own sexual subjectivities. As a constructive step in promoting dialogue about those topics, Warner decided to make a bold confessional move and to present himself as Exhibit A, as the embodiment of the problem it was crucial for gay men to solve. For on two recent occasions, and despite knowing all the risks, Warner had himself engaged in unprotected anal sex with a partner of unknown serology status—a partner who, as it turned out, though seemingly "healthy and beautiful" at the time, died a month later of AIDS-related causes (36). Warner himself, however, had not been infected with HIV by those two risky sexual encounters.

To make such a confession was obviously and deliberately to violate the long-standing ban on the gay analysis of gay affect and to expose the play of gay sexual subjectivity to the unhindered gaze of public scrutiny. Nor could confession alone promote a culture of constructive discussion, as the recent panic over barebacking—which has been fueled by a sensationalistic practice of public confession— abundantly demonstrates. So Warner approached the topic cautiously. He was highly conscious of the need to shield queer subjects, if possible, from the normalizing judgments of our psychotherapeutic culture. He therefore set out to construct an account of gay men's sexual risk-taking that would offer scant purchase for homophobia and scapegoating, that neither demonized gay men as a group nor responsibilized, culpabilized, and pathologized gay men as individuals, that did not involve a blanket disqualification of gay male eroticism in general or blame unwise behavior on some intrinsic feature of gay male psychology.[98]

Warner was determined to resist the homophobic hype of "the straight press," with its eagerness "to pin the rap on gay men, . . . to interpret gay men's desires as pathological" by telling us, in effect, "you have a tragic shortage of self-esteem, you've given up, you're irresponsible" (34). Accordingly, Warner made a strenuous effort to produce an analysis of the motives gay men might have for sexual risk-taking that deindividualized, depsychologized, and depersonalized the practice of engaging in risky sex, and he came up with a number of explanations for it that did just that—by locating its causes in a variety of cultural or practical considerations of a largely *impersonal* order—even if he occasionally reverted to psychological thinking, more deliberately at some moments than at others.

Let me say at the outset that in rehearsing Warner's explanations for some gay men's sexual risk-taking I do not mean to imply that they are correct. It is not my aim here to vindicate Warner's hypotheses, but rather to extend his style of reasoning. I do not intend to take a position on the ultimate correctness or incorrectness of Warner's interpretation, which I don't need to do for my purposes. What I want to uphold is his larger project: namely, the strategic decision to depersonalize risky sex by depsychologizing it.

❧ *The originality of* Warner's analysis lies in its attempt to look beyond such pop-psychological clichés as "survivor guilt" or "internalized homophobia" in order to locate in gay men's social worlds, rather than in our psyches, the springs for what might appear to be incomprehensible or self-destructive behavior. Warner emphasized three considerations that might be contributing to the willingness of some HIV-negative gay men to have unprotected sex: "deep identification with positive men, ambivalence about survival, and the rejection of normal life." He went on to expand on each of them, trying to distance them from psychological explanations despite the psychologizing language ("identification," "ambivalence") in which they were couched.

First, Warner noted that "being positive has become an identity," an identity that by the mid-1990s was no longer strictly associated with sickness: "positive men have developed a culture of articulacy about mortality and the expectations of 'normal life,'" and so "When negative men identify with positive men, . . . they are staking their interests with that culture and taking as their own its priorities, its mordant humor, its heightened tempo, its long view on the world." Under these circumstances, "When a negative man has unsafe sex today, it may mean not so much a gamble with the banalities of infection and disease as a way of trying on the cultural identity of the HIV-positive," the identity of those "positive friends and lovers" with whom "our own lives are bound up" (35).

Unsafe sex, in other words, might be tempting some HIV-negative men by offering them a way of expressing a sense of social and cultural solidarity with their HIV-positive comrades—an all-too-rare instance of such solidarity, to be sure, and not the most constructive one, but solidarity nonetheless. If some of us are going to be infected, as any objective look into our collective future indicates, how can we know for sure where the line between the uninfected and the infected will be drawn or what side of it we may find ourselves on? Perhaps the point is not to choose sides but to build community. At least, we can understand how a sense of group loyalty might lead some gay men to take that view, even if not all explorations of HIV-positive identity by HIV-negative men necessarily express social or political solidarity with HIV-positive people.

Second, Warner pointed out that the challenge of living with HIV/AIDS had enabled some gay men to experiment with new ways of life—and thereby to perform, in effect, a kind of practical critique of conventional norms of existence. Their example was inspiring, useful, and full of promise. Hence, Warner argued, "The identification of negative men with the culture of positive men can be liberating if it cultivates . . . the radical form of life" that the epidemic "has created for many gay men," a form of life that consists in trying to live "as a dying man does, without a belief in or sense of responsibility to the future, existing within the scope and scale of a life that may end any day" (35, quoting Odets).[99] Warner was clearly worried, though, that HIV-negative gay men would take their attraction to such a radical form of life as an incentive to be infected, that they would act out their conflicted feelings instead of interrogating them, and that they would find in "the erotic practice of risk" a means of avoiding more explicit and careful reflection on their vexed relations with their HIV-positive friends and lovers (35–36).

Third, Warner spent some time explaining what he meant by "ambivalence about survival." He pointed to the problem of despair in a world that often seemed to have written off the lives of gay men, or in which so many gay men are already infected with HIV that younger gay men might feel that such infection is unavoidable and inevitable.[100] Citing Zygmunt Bauman, Warner asked, reasonably enough, "If surviving AIDS means surviving all your positive friends and lovers, is the *you* that survives someone that you can imagine?" (36). Gay men have understandable, even creditable motives, in short, for risking infection with HIV.

All those considerations may seem to smack of psychology, but in fact they depart from a traditional psychological model of personality insofar as they form part of a larger explanatory strategy (of a classic Durkheimian kind) that consistently avoids focusing on the individual human subject and refers instead to social conditions, in this case to the particularly difficult and desperate collective situation that gay men in U.S. metropolitan centers were facing in the early 1990s.

❧ *Not content with* those social explanations, however, Warner went on to adduce considerations of a more general nature. He mentioned the age-old association of sex with death, "in part because of its sublimity," and he invoked Kant ("Mr. Responsibility himself") as a warrant for the view that "there is no sublimity without danger, without the scary ability to imagine ourselves and everything we hold dear, at least for a moment, as expendable" (35). Indeed, Warner had already noted, in his own case, that "the danger was part of the attraction," and he emphasized "the heady thrill" of the encounter itself and "how explosive the sex had been" (33).

Unsafe sex, in this light, is a way of living at the edges of cognition. It is also a kind of speculative ethical experiment, a means of playing with time that consists in putting your life at risk in the moment, in ways that may not make sense to you then and there, but that allow you to discover, retrospectively, what exactly matters to you, and why. It is, to adapt Paul Willis, "one way to make the mundane suddenly *matter*. The usual assumption of the flow of the self from the past to the future is stopped; the dialectic of time is broken."[101] Unsafe sex defies by this tactic the disciplinary logic of moral rationality itself, which requires us to evaluate our actions by orienting them towards a future: that may be a large part of its transgressive appeal. (Lauren Berlant makes a similar point about overeating as a defiant tactic of privileging laterality over teleology: "To eat can be an interruption of the desire to build toward the good life that could be a meaningful or meaningless feeling of wellbeing that spreads out for a moment, not as a projection toward a future.")[102] By putting yourself at risk, you interrupt the normal course of your life, resist its established order of meaning, and thereby perform an immanent critique of its priorities. Risk is a tactic for testing which of your values ultimately count.

Had he been given more space, Warner would have done well to expand on those ethical or philosophical considerations, because they could have displaced the mystery of risky sex from the supposedly twisted psychology of the gay male subject onto the enigma of human motivation itself. Philosophers once used to speak of the theory of moral sentiments; nowadays they tend to favor the language of "moral psychology," but the subfield of ethics designated by that term has very little do with the academic science of psychology as it is currently practiced—and so it might hold out a promising alternative.

Pursuing some traditional ethical themes, Warner might have taken up the Aristotelian topic of *akrasia* (lack of mastery or weakness of will), with its challenge to the Socratic paradox that no one errs willingly. He could have treated the Sartrean theme of vertigo, the dizzying sensation of panic that may arise from an awareness of having the freedom to make ultimate choices. Even though Warner did not have a real opportunity to put into operation his strategy of removing the question "What makes them do it?" from the realm of psychopathology to that of moral philosophy, the strategy itself was an astute one. It served both to depathologize and to de-gay the supposed conundrum of risky sex as well as to detach it from the specialized discipline of psychology by relating it to universal structures of human motivation instead of to individual motives.

❧ *Warner supplemented* his philosophical themes with some quite practical and pertinent reflections about the systematic possibilities for mixed signals in sexual communication among gay men.

Why, for example, had the other guy wanted to be fucked without a condom? . . . [T]he simplest theory: because he was already positive and wasn't worried about being infected. Usually, men who know they are positive will either tell you their status or take on themselves the burden of keeping things safe. He hadn't. But he would have been quite reasonable to think, since I went along, either that I was making my own decision or that I, too, was already positive and wasn't worried about reinfection. There were other possibilities. . . . Plenty of men, usually young, want unprotected sex because they trust the people they're with to be negative. . . . Of course, it was also possible that, like me, he was negative or didn't know his status, and was simply willing to take a risk. (34)

This example abundantly illustrates Warner's point about the need for more open, explicit, and non-judgmental discussion among gay men about HIV-serology status, acceptable levels of risk, and sexual practices. In some cases, for example, the transmission of HIV from one sexual partner to another may be the direct if inadvertent result of conflicts between different HIV/AIDS prevention strategies that have been tried at different times or in different places. Some of those strategies have emphasized the responsibility of each HIV-negative individual to safeguard his own health: it is the job of each of us, and no one else, to prevent ourselves from being infected. Other strategies have insisted on the responsibility of HIV-positive individuals to protect their partners from possible infection.

The best studies of contemporary gay male sexual practices (mostly carried out in Canada, Great Britain, and Australia, where such research can be funded) reveal the exquisite complexity of the calculations by which gay men negotiate, often quite successfully, the practical difficulties of risk reduction.[103] But those studies also delineate the systematic misunderstandings that sometimes arise from the history of conflicting prevention strategies.[104] Unprotected anal intercourse between HIV-positive and HIV-negative men can take place, for example, because some HIV-positive men may operate under the assumption (in keeping with the set of HIV/AIDS prevention protocols approved by most AIDS service organizations) that everyone is responsible for protecting himself; on that basis, they might mistakenly believe that anyone who allows himself to be fucked without a condom must already be HIV-positive and is therefore not running a risk of being infected. "Otherwise," thinks the HIV-positive man, "he wouldn't be willing to let me fuck him without a condom."

Meanwhile, some HIV-negative men may operate under the different assumption (in keeping with a different brand of HIV/AIDS prevention etiquette widespread in local gay communities) that those infected with HIV are responsible for containing the spread of the virus and should never put their partners at risk; on that basis, they might mistakenly believe that anyone who is willing to fuck without a condom must also be HIV-negative. "Otherwise," thinks the HIV-negative man, "he would surely put on a condom before fucking me." In such cases, we need not posit some kind of psychological "deficit" on the part of those men who engage in unprotected anal intercourse: they are making what they take to be an obvious and reasonable inference, using it as a tactic by which to reduce the risk of transmitting or contracting HIV. It is the larger history of HIV/AIDS prevention efforts, with their overlapping prevention paradigms and conflicting messages, of which these men are not systematically aware, that is responsible in this context for heightening the risk of HIV infection.[105]

It is also the case that tacit double-standards and panic about HIV in gay communities along with the fear of rejection and the increasing practice of serosorting itself may make some HIV-positive men reluctant to reveal their HIV-serology status to their casual sexual partners explicitly, preferring to communicate it implicitly by hints, signs, or the unavoidable if unspoken conclusion to be drawn from their own willingness to have unprotected sex. They may assume that, because the clues they drop are well known in the sexual culture of HIV-positive men, the same clues will be evident to anyone. Or they may simply hope that anyone who is willing to have unprotected sex with them is HIV-positive. HIV-negative men, by contrast, may be clueless about the hints that HIV-positive men make, ignorant of the tacit signs used in the sexual culture of HIV-positive men, willing to take a risk so long as they don't know for sure that their partner is HIV-positive, or convinced that no one who is HIV-positive would blithely offer to have unprotected sex with a stranger.[106]

Warner did not cite such common examples of sexual miscommunication to explain his own behavior, nor did he attempt to justify his lapses as the innocent results of an accidental misunderstanding. On the contrary, he was at pains to emphasize how aware he was of being in the dark, of having no idea of the exact nature of the risks he was running. Even so, his account indicates that his very uncertainty stemmed at least in part from the possibility that his partner's behavior—the fact that his partner did not insist that Warner wear a condom—might have signified (on the basis of a plausible though, as it turned out, fallacious inference) that the guy was HIV-negative. Warner may have been too morally rigorous to accept such an alibi in his own case but, whether he wanted it or not, such practical problems of communication, and the systematic misunderstandings between individuals that can arise in the context of conflicts among different HIV/AIDS prevention paradigms, did supply him with precisely such an alibi and suggested that his behavior may not simply have been impulsive or unreasoning.

Warner also refused to excuse himself on the grounds that the insertive partner in anal intercourse runs a somewhat lesser risk of HIV infection than the receptive partner, since he was aware from the start that the risk to the insertive partner from an infected receptive partner is still considerable. But such calculations do indeed figure in some gay men's risk reduction practices, and they are not entirely unreasonable since, as Warner's own case demonstrated, they sometimes work.

Kane Race, who has done some of the most sensitive and imaginative research in this area, sums up his findings (albeit for a later period when gay men had at their disposal a great deal more precise and sophisticated information about their viral load and probable degree of infectivity) as follows.

This is not a picture of people throwing caution to the wind. It is a picture of gay men appropriating medical knowledge to craft a range of considered strategies that attempt to balance sex and the avoidance of risk. These strategies are not foolproof. But many of them are scientifically plausible on the basis of epidemiological evidence, indicating a relatively informed engagement with scientific and probabilistic reasoning in gay men's sexual accounts and practice. It is not at all clear that probabilistic reasoning is always appropriate for the purposes of HIV prevention (which always involves two or more people who may be bringing different assumptions to the encounter). But . . . [t]hese strategies adapt medicine to fit the cultural desires of subjects for pleasure and safety.[107]

Warner's behavior, on this view, though risky, was not insane or suicidal.

If Warner himself did not explore the counter-rationality that might have been at work in his decision to have unprotected sex, that was surely because such a factor could not help him delve into the problem of his own subjective motivation. And it was precisely the questions of human motivation and gay subjectivity that Warner was determined to address. Motivation and subjectivity might not have been the best lenses through which to view the practice of engaging in risky sex, but Warner's insistence on anatomizing his own behavior by invoking those analytic categories is what makes his effort interesting for my purposes and particularly relevant to the larger project of exploring non-psychological approaches to the study of gay male subjectivity.

❧ *Although Warner's* analysis of gay men's sexual risk-taking was based on some of the best information available at the time, there is reason to believe that it may not be widely applicable. Since Warner's essay was written, a good deal of detailed and sensitive qualitative social research on gay men's sexual risk-taking has been carried out, and it sheds considerable light on the range of motives gay and bisexual men actually have for taking risks in their sexual practices. Kane Race, summarizing this research, points out that

> *gay men account for unsafe sex in a number of ways: erectile difficulty or frustration with condoms; getting carried away with the moment; slipping up; mistaken assumptions about one's partner's HIV status; desiring greater intimacy or intensity; particular relational dynamics (such as not wanting to compromise the encounter because of the partner's presumed superiority and/or desire for unprotected sex); not knowing how to introduce a condom; being drunk or out of it on drugs; forgetting; an accident; personal turmoil—and this is only the beginning of an interminable list, none of which are necessarily best understood as either "barebacking" or "intentional."*[108]

The distinction between intentional and unintentional acts is above all a juridical one, designed to allow the state and its institutions to differentiate those who are culpably responsible for their behavior from those who are innocent of wilful misconduct. It may well be that "intentionality" is not the right category to use for thinking about the kinds and degrees of attention or inattentiveness that we bring to our daily lives—including, especially, our sexual practices.

Lauren Berlant warns us in similar terms against construing the people we take to be the subjects of appetites "as always fully present to their motives, desires, feelings, and experiences, or as even desiring to be." As she argues, the results of clinging to such a hypercognitive model of the subject are significant: "Without attending to the varieties of constraint and unconsciousness that condition ordinary activity we persist in an attachment to a fantasy that in the truly lived life emotions are always heightened and expressed in modes of effective agency that ought justly to be and are ultimately consequential or performatively sovereign. In this habit of representing the intentional subject, a manifest lack of self-cultivating attention can easily become recast as irresponsibility, shallowness, resistance, refusal, or incapacity; and habit itself can begin to look deeply overmeaningful, such that addiction, reaction formation, conventional gesture clusters, or just being different can be read as heroic placeholders for resistance to something, affirmation of something, or a transformative desire."[109] It is our inflated conception of the intentional, cognitive subject, in other words, that leads us to exaggerate both the culpable irresponsibility of our risk-taking behavior and the heroic transgressiveness of our defiance of social norms. A more modest estimate of subjective agency would be both truer and better for us. It would, for instance, help make sense of the minimal cognition involved in sexual decision-making, including the willingness to have risky sex.

These considerations point in at least two directions. On the one hand, recent qualitative social research into gay men's sexual risk-taking confirms that portion of Warner's analysis which argues that such risk-taking is not necessarily crazy or irrational, and it supports his goal of seeking practical and social rather than psychopathological explanations for gay men's choices. On the other hand, it undermines the entire project of analyzing sexual risk in terms of individual intention, as Warner is occasionally tempted to do in ways that bolster the very model of the self-present, hypercognitive subject of sexual decision-making that Berlant criticizes. And it casts into doubt a number of Warner's grander generalizations about gay men's motivations for having risky sex, though it does not entirely exclude them either.[110]

But my point here has little to do with the rightness or wrongness of Warner's individual hypotheses, which at the very least offer eloquent testimony to his own felt experience and that of many of his friends at the time his article was written. I am interested rather in his explanatory strategy, his style of reasoning, and the political, ethical, practical, and philosophical lessons we can learn from both the successes and failures of his experiment in the social analysis of gay subjectivity. My main concern remains the possibility of creating new counter-discourses of gay sexual subjectivity that will prove to be satisfying on their own terms while refusing, for as long as may be practical, to provide a ready-made docking station for normalizing judgments and homophobic sensationalism.

IV

Warner would seem to have provided the rudiments of such a counter-discourse, a well-reasoned and searching non-psychological sketch of at least some of the subjective reasons "why gay men are having risky sex." He even came to apply his analysis to his own motives with a certain serenity, summarizing the result in an evocative phrase at the end of the article. His behavior, as he had now begun to understand it, implied that he had been willing "to think about this loss of an already necrotic world only in the practice of risk" (36).

But Warner himself did not seem to be satisfied with that explanation of his actions. Furthermore, he apparently considered his entire analysis up to that point to be insufficient, at least for some small but significant subset of gay men who have risky sex. He even regarded as seriously flawed any AIDS prevention strategy that would settle for such a limited (if suggestive) account as the one he had just provided. And so he tried out a different approach, one defined by a mode of explanation that placed greater emphasis on subjective factors.

Warner initially managed to strike a balance between introspection and social analysis. He did not leave psychic factors out of account, in other words, but he tied them to the specific social and emotional situation of gay men. He suggested that "the appeal of queer sex, for many, lies in its ability to violate the responsibilizing frames of good, right-thinking people" (35). AIDS prevention efforts that appeal to the good citizen in all of us therefore miss the point. If we were really so keen to be good citizens, we wouldn't be having so much filthy gay sex—or getting such a kick out of it. The thrill of it all comes from being naughty, disobedient, sinful, bad: things that are already *morally* risky according to the normative standards of those who do them.

AIDS prevention strategies that "see sex as a healthy expression of self-esteem and respect for others," that ignore its antisocial energies, Warner contended, do so at their peril, and at ours. For they end up repressing the very thing about sex—and about queer sex in particular—that they should be addressing: namely the intense pleasure it sometimes discovers in refusing to be "proper and good." Which is potentially quite dire, because "the queerness that is repressed in this view may be finding expression in risk" (35). What we need to confront, beyond our sexual practices, then, is the affective structure of gay male subjectivity itself, shaped by originary social experiences of rejection and shame, and bristling with impulses to transgression, which the political imperative of gay pride has made us reluctant to acknowledge and to explore.[III]

By describing our reluctance as "repression," Warner aligned his account of our resistance to the antisocial energies of sex with a psychoanalytic style of explanation. But is such an alignment necessary? Is it possible to understand the workings of gay male subjectivity, including its transgressive impulses and our political resistance to them, without recourse to psychoanalysis? Warner at least made a stab at it, which is why his effort is worth considering so closely. Despite his talk of repression, and despite his even more ominous invocation of the unconscious, he continued to think about sex as a social, or antisocial, phenomenon. If, he argued, it is the transgressive nature of queerness itself that finds expression in risk, and if risk enhances the sublimity of sex, then "the pursuit of dangerous sex is not as simple as mere thrill seeking, or self-destructiveness. It may represent deep and mostly unconscious thinking about desire and the conditions that make life worthwhile" (35).

Despite this rhetoric of psychic depth, Warner was still

trying to distance his explanation of risky sex from a psychoanalytic one. The telling phrase here is "unconscious thinking." The Freudian unconscious does not think, much less does it think "about the conditions that make life worthwhile." That sounds like traditional ethical reflection of an almost Kantian sort, a meditation about proper values and the definition of the good life. The psychoanalytic unconscious is not a Kantian philosopher.

What Warner seems to have had in mind here is his own very careful account of the decidedly non-psychoanalytic considerations that might contribute to HIV-negative gay men's willingness to engage in risky sex—namely, their "deep identification with positive men, ambivalence about survival, and rejection of normal life." Gay men may not be aware of acting from those motives: in that sense, those motives are unconscious. But they are unconscious not because they spring from drives that are inaccessible to consciousness; they are unconscious simply because the sexual actors who are animated by those motives are not aware of them, and so they do not recognize the logic behind their actions for what it really is.[112] The problem is one of cognition (in the sense of self-awareness), not psychology.

Gay men are not exactly irrational, on this account. Rather, they act for specifiable reasons—or out of a commitment to certain values—which however are not always available to them as matters of conscious, explicit, deliberative reflection. Gay men's motives for having risky sex, Warner implied, spring from the unresolved emotional and social ambivalence of their lives. They arise from systematically divided loyalties, from unrationalized or unanalyzed experiences of social contradiction. The solution is to be sought not in therapy but in the kind of explicit and deliberative ethical reflection that Warner's own article exemplified. The tensions in gay men's ethical lives need to be worked through, by means of rigorous, practical analysis of a social and institutional kind, and opportunities have to be created for working through them in shared, communal, counterpublic spheres. By means of such reasoning, Warner succeeded in providing a "deeper" answer to the question of why gay men have risky sex, and he was able to extend his non-normalizing account of risk-taking to the affective realm of gay male life without routing it through psychology or psychoanalysis.

❧ *In the end,* however, Warner did not manage to sustain that essentially social and ethical analysis of gay male subjectivity, with its multitude of original and imaginative insights into the collective emotional plight of U.S. urban-dwelling gay men in the face of the HIV/AIDS crisis of the early 1990s. One of the many reasons for refusing a psychoanalytic approach to the topic, after all, had been precisely to avoid depoliticizing gay subjectivity's relation to the larger social collectivity that frames homosexual desire, and Warner's explanatory strategy was designed to foreground the connections between gay men's sexual ethics and their specific social and political situations. Unfortunately, without apparently noticing the slippage in his argument, Warner came to align his own social, collective, cognitive, non-psychoanalytic notion of the unconscious with the more frankly psychoanalytic conception of it invoked by the distinguished queer theorist and leading AIDS activist Douglas Crimp. "Most people only have pop psychology for thinking about sex," Warner quoted Crimp as saying. "Only if you can acknowledge that you have an unconscious can you admit doing self-destructive things without just feeling guilty" (35).

Warner treated that statement as a mere expansion of his own claim that "the pursuit of dangerous sex is not as simple as mere . . . self-destructiveness . . . [and] may represent deep and mostly unconscious thinking about desire and the conditions that make life worthwhile." But it is clear that what Crimp called "*an* unconscious" is very different from what Warner meant by "mostly unconscious thinking." Warner's notion referred to an unrecognized, inexplicit working through of the social and ethical con-

tradictions in the individual's life world, whereas Crimp
was simply invoking the psychic entity theorized by Freud.
Crimp, then, treated the unconscious not as the absence of
rigorous social and institutional analysis, à la Warner, but
as an independent psychic force—observing, senten-
tiously, "We all fail to realize how powerful the unconscious is" (35).

Like Warner, Crimp wanted to avoid personalizing
risky sex. If he emphasized the power of unconscious
drives that human beings cannot control or even understand, that is because he was trying to shift the blame away
from the putatively defective psychology of individuals,
who would otherwise have become personally answerable
for their inward failings—as in the facile, pathologizing
charges of "self-destructiveness" and "internalized homophobia"—and would thereby have found themselves
newly responsibilized and culpabilized for their behavior.[113] The strategy here was to use psychoanalysis to free
gay men from psychology, from a psychological culture of
guilt, in order to promote the kind of open dialogue about
sex, risk, and HIV/AIDS that could generate new and
more effective prevention strategies.

For if we feel merely guilty as individuals, we won't
want to admit that we take risks, or so the argument goes,
and even if we do admit that we take them, we will only
talk about them in the idiom of personal blame and self-
condemnation—an idiom exemplified by the sometimes
punitive rhetoric that Warner used in his article to casti-
gate his own risk-taking. That refusal to address openly
and dispassionately our collective practices of risk would
fatally inhibit candid, honest, non-judgmental communication about the sexual behavior we actually engage in and
the degrees of risk we are collectively willing to accept. A
psychoanalytic acknowledgment of the force of the unconscious, by contrast, would enable us to confront our
actions and own up to them without necessarily taking
personal blame for them, or dwelling in an incapacitating
state of guilt because of them, since it is not our ego that is

responsible for them. It would thereby facilitate a frank and constructive dialogue. As a gay AIDS prevention activist quoted by Warner says, "If I can't talk honestly about what it means to me to have someone's dick up my butt or to have someone come in my mouth, I can't think through what it would cost me to give it up" (36).

But despite that rigorous and admirable effort to prevent psychoanalytic concepts from functioning "as a kind of tool for establishing the intelligibility of a given sexual pleasure and, thus, gauging it in terms of normality," as Foucault once put it,[114] Crimp and Warner were ultimately unwilling or unable to stave off the pathologizing effects of their chosen interpretative strategy. It is not so easy after all to detach psychoanalytic reasoning from normative thinking. Normalizing judgments have a way of sneaking back in and reasserting themselves, as we shall see, even within the queerest critical deployments of psychoanalysis.

❧ *In trying to* explain to himself, and to us, why he took sexual risks, Warner was confronting an explanatory difficulty now familiar to generations of gay men. Unprotected anal sex, according to the terms in which many gay men describe their motives for engaging in it, is very often not a matter of "intention," as Kane Race has suggested. But if it is not intentional, what is it, exactly? Is it *unintentional*? Warner's account of his experience does not make that sound like a good description either. Do the terms *intentional* and *unintentional* exhaust the range of possible explanations? Or is there some third term that can mediate between them, that would be consistent with each of them? It is this very conundrum, this paradoxical problem of intentionality and agency, that makes a psychoanalytic account appealing—especially to those audiences who may not have the patience for the conceptual nuances that Lauren Berlant's social approach to theorizing intentionality and agency offers. Psychoanalysis in this context provides some obvious solutions. The "unconscious," for example, is neither intentional nor unintentional, neither an expression of the self (in the sense of the ego) nor wholly extraneous to the self.

From the outset of his article, Warner had in fact flirted with a model of human motivation that represents individual actions as the surface effects of underlying and largely inaccessible drives: "What *makes* some men fuck without protection when they 'know better'?" he had asked (33; emphasis added). The very form of that now-familiar question already presumed some sort of separate principle of causation or compulsion in the gay male subject, a potentially terrifying split in the subject's agency. That does not necessarily mean that Warner's approach to risky sex was imbued from the start with psychoanalytic ways of thinking: not all accounts of cognitive dissonance depend, after all, on depth psychology or a theory of psychic drives. It was precisely in order to convey his experience of inner division without committing himself to a theoretical position on the topic of human motivation that Warner resorted to a startling metaphor instead of an analytic category in describing his apparently ungovernable impulse to have unprotected sex at a particular moment with a particular individual. "I recoiled so much from what I had done that it seemed to be not my choice at all. A mystery, I thought. A monster did it" (33).

That was not a casual or a careless remark. Warner insisted on the imagery of demonic possession as a way of getting around the paradox of an unintentional intention. He was trying to articulate the experience of internal alterity, the sense of being taken over by uncontrollable, irrational, and destructive forces from within the self.[115] When he found that his panic at having risked infecting himself once was not sufficient to prevent him from having unprotected sex again with the same partner, he recurred to his earlier metaphor in the course of relating the incident: "The next time I saw the same man, I thought to myself to take precautions, but I could tell by the heady thrill that my monster was in charge." Given Warner's obvious fondness for this B-movie allegory, it's no wonder that he represented himself as telling himself, in the language of teen horror flicks, "Be afraid. Be very afraid" (33).

Warner's demonology was a deliberately chosen strata-gem for conveying to his readership the central, most audacious, risky, and supposedly profound point of his entire article—namely, that the sort of HIV/AIDS educa-tion that "calls for people to affirm life and see sex as a healthy expression of self-esteem and respect for others" is barking up the wrong tree, powerless to confront the anti-social impulses that drive gay men to have unsafe sex. "One campaign from the San Francisco AIDS Foundation urges men to treat sex the way you might buy municipal bonds: 'Playing it safe, making a plan, and sticking to it.' Most efforts to encourage us to take care of ourselves through safer sex also invite us to pretend that our only desire is to be proper and good" (35). Try telling *that* to your inner monster.

The real problem with standard HIV/AIDS prevention efforts, it turns out, is that they do not confront the mys-terious depths in the gay male subject where the impulse to have risky sex originates. Attempts to build HIV/AIDS prevention on appeals to self-esteem miss their target because they are directed at the decent, law-abiding, healthy gay individual who has no need to be persuaded, and would never dream of having risky sex anyway, while they have no ability to restrain the antisocial monster inside him, the force that can drive this otherwise well-behaved person to violate his consciously espoused beliefs and values. Only a model of gay male subjectivity that allows for sources of motivation in the subject other than the ego can accommodate the unpalatable truth. And what is that truth, according to Michael Warner? "Abjection continues to be our dirty secret" (35).

Warner's monster, then, had at least two aspects. First, far from being a psychoanalytic metaphor, it functioned as a phenomenological description. It was intended to convey what Warner's own experience of acting against his better judgment felt like to him. It dramatized his sensation of

losing mastery over himself and his behavior, of undergo-
ing a deep, internal split. Second, it served as a figure for
the antisocial impulse to queer revolt that may lead some
gay men to have risky sex—the delirious pleasure some gay
men may take in contravening both society's norms and
their own ("the rejection of normal life"). Both of those
dimensions are compatible with a social analysis of the sort
that Warner had intended to provide. But when the trope
of the inner monster comes to express and to stand in for
Douglas Crimp's view (approved by Warner) about the
sublime power of the unconscious, then the monster starts
to shade into a Freudian allegory, and that is where the real
trouble begins.

The implication of Warner's argument now seems to be
that blandly ego-fortifying efforts to prevent the transmission of HIV go wrong because they mistake what risky sex
is all about. In fact, they conspire to deny and repress it.
Risky sex is not an affair of the ego: it is not about
affirming life, asserting yourself, having fun, being happy,
loving yourself. In that sense, it will remain incomprehensible so long as we insist on identifying the self entirely
with the ego—so long as we refuse to confront, in other
words, the force of the unconscious. Warner's interpretation ultimately yields a picture of human motivation in
general, and gay male subjectivity in particular, that makes
a sharp distinction between conscious and unconscious
wishes, between the ego and the id, pegging the success of
efforts at HIV/AIDS prevention on their ability to address
the unconscious psychic forces that allegedly drive at least
some gay men, despite their best intentions, to take risks in
their sexual practices.

But it is not clear from Warner's article what HIV prevention strategies that *did* take into account the power of
the unconscious would look like. How, one might wonder,
could a prevention campaign addressed to uninfected gay
men manage to target and to neutralize the multitude of
individual, unconscious promptings that supposedly drive

such men to have risky sex? Fortunately, though, Warner's self-analysis already contained hints of a possible way out of this apparent impasse, indications of a non-psychoanalytic alternative to the Freudian allegory that would result from interpreting his demonic metaphor in psychic terms.

❧ *Let us return* to Warner's enigmatic claim that "abjection continues to be our dirty secret." Abjection, then, is what we need to talk about, when we talk about what it means to have someone's dick up our butts or to have someone come in our mouths. We need to admit our pleasure in being the lowest of the low, in being bad, in being outlaws, in betraying both our own values and those of the people around us. And we need to do so non-judgmentally, without having to berate ourselves for a weak ego, for a lack of self-esteem, or for some other kind of distinctively *psychological* failure. Only an account of abjection that bypasses the paradox of intentionality, that refuses to present queer motivation in terms of either hypercognitive rational agency or irrational, incomprehensible, helpless compulsion, can capture and make sense of the antisocial, transgressive appeal of risky sex—an appeal that can allegedly exert such monstrous power over gay men.

Now does that in fact mean that we have to commit ourselves to a psychoanalytic model of interiority? Will only psychoanalysis enable us to make sense of our motivations, to address the vicissitudes of abjection? Is there no other way of inquiring guiltlessly into the affective workings of the gay male subject? Can nothing but a psychoanalytic insistence on the power of the unconscious enable us to resolve the paradox of an impulse to have risky sex that is neither intentional nor unintentional? After all, one problem with a psychoanalytic approach, as Warner's example showed, is that although it may avoid personalizing unsafe sex, it does not avoid pathologizing—literally, demonizing—gay men. Nor can a narrow fixation on the power of the unconscious allow for the determining influence of that complex array of concrete social factors whose operation Warner himself had so meticulously analyzed.

The reception of Warner's article provides eloquent testimony to the perils involved in any attempt to renew an inquiry into queer affect or gay subjectivity. The article was acclaimed, not surprisingly, by an unholy congregation of right-wing Christian evangelists and psychoanalytically-minded queer theorists. The former were pleased to see their view of homosexual sinfulness vindicated by what they took to be Warner's confession that every gay man has a monster inside him. The latter exploited Warner's candor in order to argue that "gay men's unsafe sex has less to do with lack of education than with the unconscious": that is, with "a passion for ignorance."[116] As an account of the particular challenges that HIV/AIDS education campaigns face in the context of a complex, constantly evolving history of prevention efforts as well as a gay male sexual culture that repeatedly adapts itself to new and changing medical realities, neither approach seems very astute or very useful.

When it is seen in this light, Warner's flirtation with gay demonology abundantly explains (and nearly justifies) the post-Stonewall policy of imposing a blackout on gay inquiries into the internal dynamics of gay subjectivity. After all, it hardly seems unreasonable for the lesbian and gay movement to have wanted to close off the category of gay subjectivity from the possibility of gay investigation, to worry about what such investigations might disclose, and whether such disclosures would be used against us, when an inquiry into gay subjectivity by even so deliberate, intelligent, principled, and politically savvy a thinker as Michael Warner could result in the dangerous (if exciting) notion that inside every gay man lurks an uncontrollable, sex-crazed, antisocial monster. Admittedly, if we take a psychoanalytic view of the matter, we have to allow that the same thing is in theory true of everyone, straight or gay, since everyone is supposed to have an unconscious, according to Freudian doctrine. But lesbians and gay men might be forgiven for presuming that we are the ones who will somehow end up footing the bill for that allegedly universal monstrosity, especially when it is interpreted to mean that "gay men's unsafe sex has less to do with lack of education than with the unconscious."[117]

Even gay psychoanalytic theorists, like Tim Dean (the author of the pronouncement just quoted), do not hesitate to consider "the challenges of safe-sex education in relation to the death drive." They do not hesitate to invoke that Freudian concept in order to argue against "the simplistic notion, prevalent in so many studies of homophobia, that the harm done gay people has a purely external source. . . . Consideration of the death drive allows us to conceptualize a nonexternal force that works against the subject (that is, against the subject's well-being), yet which cannot be characterized as the effect of any internalization."[118]

Gay people, in other words, need to reckon, on this account, with the power of a monstrous force that works against us from within—and thus with the possibility that we are our own worst enemies. That we are also victims of homophobic violence, both material and symbolic, to say nothing of a dangerous virus, does not let us off the hook, according to Dean, since all that has to do with "a purely external source." HIV/AIDS prevention efforts that take the virus to be the enemy therefore miss the real problem, which has to do with the monstrous force allegedly internal to us, more dangerous than any microbe or any social policy.

Now, such a force is in theory at work within everyone, not just gay people, since the Freudian death drive is universal. But gay men are the ones whose sexual behavior is currently the object of particular, punitive scrutiny, just as it is gay men whose sexual risk-taking in the context of the HIV/AIDS epidemic is being cited as evidence for the power of the death drive. This style of psychoanalytic reasoning endows the death drive with both a grossly literal and a homosexually specific application. So if it is the death drive that is the cause of gay male risk-taking and the key to our sexual subjectivity, and if the only way to talk honestly about the meaning of gay male sexual practices is to invoke the psychoanalytic category of the unconscious or to confront the urgings of the death drive—if, indeed, that is our only hope of stopping the spread of HIV/AIDS—we are all in a lot of trouble.

V

How can we think about gay male subjectivity, including its seamier dimensions, without either inviting the accusation of pathology or aggressively defending ourselves against it (by insisting, for example, that gay is good)? How can we begin to think about gay subjectivity on its own terms? Let us return to Warner's unpalatable truth, and take it up once again, in a less impassioned and more exploratory frame of mind.

Abjection, Warner said, is our dirty secret. Let's suppose, for the sake of argument, that Warner was correct. What then? Does an acknowledgment of the centrality of abjection in the formation of the gay male subject entail a comparable centrality for psychoanalysis as a privileged mode of gay self-interrogation? Can only psychoanalysis reveal to us the unpalatable but inescapable truth of gay male subjectivity? Will nothing but psychoanalysis enable us to confront our antisocial impulses and thereby save us from ourselves? Well, that all depends on how we understand "abjection."

In her 1980 book-length discussion of abjection, *Powers of Horror,* Julia Kristeva did speak about abjection in a psychoanalytic idiom, though she also explored it via anthropology, religion, and literature. Abjection for Kristeva is a kind of splitting or crisis in the self, whereby one violently casts out of the self something that is so much a part of the self that one can never succeed in getting rid of it. Abjection is an extreme form of disidentification. The abject is neither subject nor object, but something of one's own for which one feels horror and revulsion, as if it were unclean, filthy, rotten, disgusting, spoiled, impure—such that any

69

contact with it becomes contaminating, nauseating, defiling. Corpses, for example, or shit; frequently, for Kristeva, the maternal body.[119] Or homosexual desire.

Kristeva never mentions homosexuality; she virtually never even alludes to it. But one could in fact extend Kristeva's account—which is in the first instance phenomenological, or descriptive, not psychoanalytic—to homosexuality (even though, unlike most of the things we abject, according to the examples that Kristeva cites, homosexuality is not a material substance). Gay men after all are "abjected," in Kristeva's sense, by straight society. More to the point, homosexuality itself can be a perennial source of abjection for some gay men, a source of horror and revulsion, because it is universally abominated, considered abnormal and perverted, and some gay men take those judgments against homosexuality to heart from a young age. Indeed, even to recognize oneself as being named, described, and summed up by the clinical term *homosexual* (or *faggot* or *queer*) is to come to self-awareness and to a recognition of social condemnation at the very same instant.[120] Abjection therefore has a particularly precise and powerful relevance to gay men as well as to other despised social groups, who have a heightened, and intimate, experience of its social operations.

Gay subjectivity is divided against itself, formed in stigma, in rejection by others—especially by those whom one desires—and by oneself. Our very loves and pleasures are constituted in relation to parts of ourselves that are causes of irredeemable shame in our social experience of them. In the era of gay pride, moreover, such shame is the occasion for further shame. That is what Warner meant when he referred to abjection as our "dirty secret." He was talking about our sense of deep inner unworthiness, which gay pride paradoxically can sometimes compound and reinforce.

Even on this account, however, abjection does not originate in psychic causes. It is the consequence of society's collective judgment against us. Its vicissitudes are not those of an unconscious instinct but of social death—the annihilating experience of exclusion from the world of decent people. Abjection is an effect of the play of social power. It describes the shape of gay men's relations to their world. Those relations structure the subjective life of homosexuality; in that sense, they could be described in terms of social psychology. But rather than represent the effects of the struggle between the gay subject and the social world in a one-way, static fashion—as psychological damage, as the infliction of a psychic wound—the concept of abjection presents that struggle in dialectical, dynamic fashion as an ongoing battle for meaning. Abjection is not a normative notion, not an index of psychological health, but a way of imagining and figuring social relations and their subjective vicissitudes.

Hence, abjection does not represent a key concept in the writings of either Freud or Lacan (although Lacan at least invokes it a dozen times in his published writings and seminars, mostly to badmouth other psychoanalysts with whom he disagrees—by dismissing them, contemptuously, as "abject").[121] Abjection does not originate in psychoanalysis, and it has little basis in it. It does boast an impeccable pedigree in French thought, extending back well beyond Kristeva. But that pedigree is not psychoanalytic. It is queer.

Not only does that tradition of queer thought hold out an alternative to psychoanalysis. It also offers a compelling, homegrown, non-psychological and non-psychoanalytic model of gay subjectivity. All the more reason for queers to give it serious consideration before rushing to conceptualize abjection in psychoanalytic terms.

❧ *Abjection reaches* back from Kristeva to the existentialist philosopher Jean-Paul Sartre. In 1952 Sartre, though avowedly heterosexual himself, lavished meticulous attention on the topic of gay abjection in the course of a seven-hundred-page introduction to the collected works of Jean Genet, entitled *Saint Genet,* which he dedicated to a series of reflections on the social phenomenology of homosexuality and crime.[122] From there, abjection can be traced back to Genet himself, who used the word occasionally in his early writings, starting with his first novel, *Our Lady of the Flowers,* in 1942, before making it into a leitmotif of his 1948 memoir, *The Thief's Journal.* Genet himself probably got the notion of abjection from the work of his acquaintance Marcel Jouhandeau, a voluminously prolific, violently anti-Semitic, right-wing, Catholic writer, who was also a gay man, and who seems to have derived the term from Christian spirituality. For Jouhandeau, homosexuality served as a vehicle for experiencing, in a perverse imitation of Christ, the contempt of the world. Jouhandeau catalogued the social vicissitudes to which homosexual desire subjected him in a remarkable, influential, and now-forgotten book, published anonymously in 1939, and never translated into English, called *De l'abjection* ("On Abjection").[123] So that is where our story begins.

For Jouhandeau, abjection was a social concept rather than a psychological one. That much is clear from the title of the book's opening chapter, "In the Presence of Others" *(En présence des autres).* It begins, "I am sometimes the victim of an incomprehension, of a spontaneous aversion on the part of men, even of strangers, which ends by relegating me to permanent exile. Some people find my presence on this earth suspect, and their hostile attitude throws me back upon my Secret. But nothing exalts me more surely than reprobation."[124] After about 150 pages of this sort of thing, consisting of fragmentary coming-out stories, bits of perverse theology, aphorisms, erotic reveries, and prayers, comes a final chapter, entitled "Praise of Abjection" *(Éloge de l'abjection),* in which Jouhandeau celebrates the transformative if agonizing effects of social humiliation. He dilates on the "happiness of being abused," on the "revelation" that results from "insults and public contempt": "You are quite possibly no longer the person you thought you were. You are no longer the person you knew, but the person that other people thought they knew, thought they recognized as this sort of person or that. . . . You try at first to pretend that it's not true, that it's only a mask, a theatrical costume that they have clothed you in so as to mock you, and you want to tear off that mask, that costume, but no—they cling to you so closely that it is your own face, your own flesh and yourself that you are in fact tearing to pieces in the effort to get rid of them" (161).

Instead of throwing off that costume, Jouhandeau assumed it. He discovered "happiness in everything that isolates me, that 'abjects' me" (164). This happiness is not simply a pleasure in surrender and self-abasement, although it also is that. It is rather what we might call an existential survival strategy. As Jouhandeau says, "I am like someone whom another has got hold of by the hair and who, not wishing to give out that appearance, pretends he is being caressed" (166: *Je suis comme un qu'un autre tiendrait par les cheveux et qui, n'en voulant pas avoir l'air, feindrait d'être caressé*). Jouhandeau's happiness in abjection was not something that he intended, but neither is it something that merely happened to him. It was not a matter of intention at all. It was a transformative experience that he did not set out to have but in which he nonetheless participated, with startling and unanticipated results. The effect of his perversion, he discovered, was to lead him, through the experience of abjection, on a path exactly parallel to that of sainthood—though in the opposite direction (165).

That was also Genet's central theme. Sainthood after all was his goal.[125] In *Miracle of the Rose* (1943), Genet improved on Jouhandeau by aspiring to a sainthood that took the opposite route from the conventional one, a sainthood that consisted not in an ascent to heaven but in the "abjection" of being driven down into the darkness of crime and perversion—a degradation in the literal, etymological sense of the word. Even in this degraded form, however, sainthood achieves the same effect as conventional holiness. It enables the individual to break out of ordinary life, to transcend the social. As Sartre commented, "Sainthood is in its essence anti-social": it removes the individual, for better or for worse, from the normal human order.[126] The pariah, like the saint, is no longer subject to all the usual rules, no longer governed by the regime of the normal. He has escaped, slipped the bonds of conventional sociality, through the very extremity of his degradation and misfortune.

Abjection was Genet's name for this involuntary, inverted sainthood that, like all sainthood in his conception, is not chosen but imposed by force of circumstance (a power that Genet identified with the power of God).[127] But just because abjection is not chosen, or intentional, does not mean that it doesn't require work, or that the abjected individual contributes nothing to his own abjection. On the contrary. For Genet, as Sartre noted, abjection is an "ascesis," a spiritual labor, which blazes the path to sainthood.[128] And, like sainthood, abjection is both martyrdom and triumph at once: it elevates even as it humiliates. Genet accordingly celebrated the abjected individual's capacity to find in the lowest depths of degradation a miraculous salvation. The exact nature and functioning of the switch-point between degradation and salvation remained mysterious to Genet: that is why he presented it as miraculous. But however it worked, abjection held out the possibility of transcending social humiliation and attaining, at considerable personal cost, to a perverse exaltation.

The best illustration of abjection in this sense can be found in the famous scene at the end of *Miracle of the Rose,* in which a group of boys at the reformatory of Mettray torment another boy called Bulkaen by forcing him to stand several yards away from them with his mouth open while they take turns trying to spit into it (316–20). Genet himself did not witness this horrible competition. He was not even in Mettray at the time. Another boy who knew that Genet had been in love with Bulkaen (and who was in love with Genet himself) maliciously recounted the episode to Genet, thinking it would lower Bulkaen in Genet's eyes, making him into an object of derision and contempt. But Bulkaen's shame only inspired Genet to identify with him, to love him even more.

What is remarkable about Genet's account of Bulkaen's ordeal is its mode of narration. Genet decided to tell the story in the first person, from his own point of view, as if he had personally suffered Bulkaen's abominable fate himself. He wanted to make Bulkaen's abjection his own. The humility of that gesture was proportional to its grandiosity. By taking Bulkaen's place, Genet was both abasing himself and glorifying himself, with the outrageous result that he could compare his sacrifice to Jesus Christ's. "As others once took upon themselves the sin of mankind, I'm going to take upon myself that excess of horror which Bulkaen was made to bear" (317). Genet's appropriation of the persecuted boy's subject position, his imaginative substitution of himself for Bulkaen at the moment of the latter's social annihilation, was both an ethical experiment and an act of love—a way of testing whether abjection could be imaginatively shared and, if it could be, whether the sharing of abjection might give rise to an erotic solidarity among the abused and rejected.

Genet allowed that Bulkaen was pathetic—that "Bulkaen was shame itself" (320). But he wished to join him in the very depths of that shame, to overcome the isolation which the concerted act of humiliation had been designed to inflict on Bulkaen, and to reclaim him for a larger imagined community of the outcast (*notre groupe de réprouvés*: 317).[129] "Since I love him, I have to love him *because* of it, so as to leave no possible opportunity for contempt, nor disgust. . . . I loved Bulkaen for his ignominy" (315–16).

Genet's love took the specific form of speaking from the perspective of Bulkaen himself so as to reconstitute and to relive the subjective experience of his "execution" (317). He described how "I" was accosted by the gang, how the world around "me" suddenly turned into a hell where "every tree, flower, bee, the blue sky, the grass" became accessory to "my" terror and seemed to have no other object but "my" torment (317). He told how "I" had involuntarily swallowed the first gob of spit that landed in "my" mouth. As the torture intensified in its cruelty, Genet's vicarious experience of annihilation began to warp under the awful pressure of it. "It would have taken very little to transform this atrocious game into a chivalric one, such that instead of spit I would be covered with a shower of roses. For inasmuch as the motions were the same, fate would not have had to go to much trouble in order to change everything: the group forms . . . some boys make motions of throwing . . . it wouldn't have cost much for the outcome to be happiness. . . . I prayed God to ease His intention a little, to make a false movement so that the boys would no longer hate me, would love me." As the gang drew nearer, as their murderous excitement increased, their victim attained in his imagination an exalted gravity: "I was no longer an adulteress to be stoned but an object employed in a rite of love. I desired that they would spit at me more, with thicker viscosities" (319).

🌹 *The alchemical* transmutation of social humiliation into erotico-religious glorification is not a matter of psychology here, except in the trivial sense that it takes place in the inner life of the individual. To say this is not to insist on some anti-psychological dogma. It is simply to register the striking and distinctive features of Genet's text—to offer a factual description of it. Genet studiously avoids using psychological language. He provides a vivid, moving account of Bulkaen's subjectivity, indeed a memorable account, but one that is psychically empty. That is an important part of what makes his writing so original, so much what it is. Genet gives us a picture of subjectivity without psychology.

The sudden vision of happiness produced in Genet by the experience of social humiliation is not the unconscious working out of some childhood trauma, nor is it a symptom of a sexual perversion (defined in psychological or psy-

choanalytic terms as a deviation from healthy functioning).[130] After all, at least as it figures within the aesthetic
design of his narrative, the trauma in question was not
even Genet's own. It happened to someone else, not to
him. Far from constituting the sort of individualizing
trauma that results in unique psychic damage, abjection
registers and describes the generalized effects of social
oppression, which in Genet's case consisted in the social
injuries of sexuality and class—the operations of the order
of normality itself. Which is why Genet was able to share
Bulkaen's experience of abjection in the first place. *The
arena in which the struggle takes place is not the psyche but the
field of social power.* The human subject is part of that field.

Genet's exaltation was a response to mainstream society's concerted attempt at degradation. It expressed existential resistance to the experience of being socially dominated.[131] If Genet was able to participate in Bulkaen's
abjection, which he did not so much as even witness, that
is because Genet was familiar from the vicissitudes of his
own social existence with the unintended effects produced
in the degraded individual by humiliation—with the ways
that such humiliation can stimulate an instinct of defiance.
In the unpredictable course of its efforts to abject the
pariah, society suddenly loses its annihilating power over
its victim; his fear and horror are turned into resistance,
even into desire. That dawning sense of subjective escape
from persecution, that intimation of a possible line of
flight, is what generates a sense of exaltation. It is less a
matter of triumphing over your adversaries than a process
of making yourself unfindable by those who would destroy
you—through discovering in the very act of surrender and
abasement the erotic and spiritual means of your own
transformation and transfiguration.[132]

That is how abjection works, or how it is imagined to
work, according to Genet. That is how it produces in
social pariahs an inverse saintliness. Genet's writing,
though highly idiosyncratic, is worthy of careful consideration because it provides "a touchstone by which to estab-

lish the limits of psychoanalytic explanation," as Sartre astutely pointed out.[133] Abjection, as Genet understood it, describes a dynamic social process constitutive of the subjectivity of gay men and other inferiorized groups. Abjection is not unique to gay men, but it doesn't have to be in order to furnish a compelling account of gay male behavior.

The social and subjective experience of abjection is reflected at a great distance, and caricatured, by psychology and psychoanalysis, which install in its place only a kind of pop-abjection called masochism. But to interpret abjection in psychological or psychoanalytic terms as masochism, and thus as a *perversion,* is to shatter the bonds of love and solidarity that Genet's narrative forges among the abject. It is to mistake the work of freedom, as Sartre argued, for evidence of psychopathology.

"The language of psychiatry," Foucault once said, "is a monologue of reason *about* madness."[134] Genet did not try to interrupt that monologue. Instead, and over against it, he invented the homosexual subject. That is, he created a literary discourse in which homosexuality speaks and in which the subjective life of male homosexuality achieves a non-psychological representation. In place of psychological science, gay subjectivity.[135]

To interpret as masochism Genet's determination to convert his social objectification into queer subjectivity is also to deny the possibility that abjection may eventuate in an escape from persecution. By "masochism" here I do not refer to the sexual practice that consists in making strategic use of pain in order to intensify erotic sensation, to amplify it to the point of ecstasy. Nor do I have in mind the communal, subcultural identities and movements that define themselves through their shared skillfulness at wielding those techniques. Rather, by "masochism" I denote the normative psychological and psychiatric concept, which designates a sexual aberration or perversion, an abnormal or pathological condition of the individual subject. The difference between masochism in this sense and abjection is that masochism designates the unhealthy enjoyment of pain and humiliation, whereas abjection consists in a kind of neutralization of their power through a reversal of the social relations of force.

Abjection is not about crossing a threshold beyond which pain turns into pleasure. It is not about the enjoyment of being dominated. Far from glorifying domination, abjection achieves a spiritual release from it by <u>derealizing its humiliating effects</u>—by depriving domination of its ability to demean the subject and, thus, robbing it of a portion of its reality. As a result, social persecution loses some of its crushing power and changes its meaning (hatred is transformed into love). Only once domination has been defied through being resignified can it be transformed into a vehicle for attaining beatitude. Genet does not enjoy his suffering: he is miraculously saved from it.

By contrast, masochism, as a psychologically normalizing concept, refuses to allow for the queer possibility of salvation that Genet describes. It does not acknowledge that those who hurt you may not in fact be able to harm you; instead, it insists on attributing to them real, irresistible power over you, implying that to be mistreated is always to be damaged and that to derive any pleasure from such mistreatment is simply to enjoy in perverted fashion the horrible things they do to you.

The psychological concept of masochism expresses in this way heterosexual culture's unshakable faith in the efficacy of its own power to persecute, its conviction that its victims really are destroyed when it tries to destroy them, and that our occasional ability to slip through the web of those inflictions—by finding a source of exaltation and personal transfiguration in an oblique relation to the very suffering they would cause us—is not a creative response to social violence, is not a testimony to the power of queer fantasy, is not a possible basis for queer solidarity, but just another sign that there is [something deeply wrong with us.]

abjection.

When heterosexual culture insists in this presumptuous way on the inescapability of social power, it effectively forecloses the possibility of that power's productive reversal—and of the corresponding empowerment to be found by those inferiorized individuals who somehow take the very substance of humiliation and forge from it the stuff of a paradoxical exaltation.[136] As Genet put it, in a densely epigrammatic metaphor, "My pride takes its royal hue from the purple of my shame" *(Mon orgueil s'est coloré avec la pourpre de ma honte).*[137]

Abjection involves a kind of engagement with the very process of humiliation, a struggle with it that sometimes leads to a transmutation of it, thereby disclosing unexpected opportunities for transcending its degradation and surmounting its terror. Not only is abjection *not* identical to masochism, then: the very category of masochism represents the denial—one might even say the political prohibition—that such a thing as Genet's abjection is possible.

🌺 *The word abjection* itself does not occur in Genet's narrative of the spitting scene from *Miracle of the Rose,* only in his reflections on sainthood which immediately precede it. For a more explicit and sustained exploration of abjection, as Genet understood it, and for a clearer demonstration of the distinction between abjection and the psychological concept of masochism, we have to turn to the opening pages of *The Thief's Journal,* a work that consists in an extended dialogue between shame and pride.[138]

It is here that Genet describes how the experience of abjection confronted him with the existential necessity of taking a bitter pleasure in humiliation, of crazily glorying in it, since only by that means could he resist its soul-destroying effects. Unlike the spitting scene in *Miracle of the Rose,* the sort of abjection on display in this early chapter of *The Thief's Journal* is grimly impersonal: it springs from the profound misery of social degradation and exclusion, and there is little about it that could be considered sexy. Living destitute in Spain as a beggar and a prostitute, at the age of twenty, Genet became acquainted with what he called "the stateliness of abjection *(les fastes de l'abjection)*. . . . Though I may be unable to describe its mechanism to you, at least I can say that I slowly forced myself to consider that wretched life a chosen necessity. Never did I try to make of it something other than what it was, I did not try to adorn it, to mask it; I wanted rather to affirm it precisely in its sordidness, and the most sordid tokens became for me tokens of grandeur."[139]

By way of an example, Genet tells the story of how he was picked up and arrested by the police, who hauled him off to jail, where they emptied his pockets and found on him a half-used tube of vaseline—and mentholated vaseline at that. "So, you take it up the nose, do you?" scoffs the police officer, triggering a round of general mockery, in which Genet himself dolefully participates. From this follows a crucial pronouncement. "Amid the elegant objects taken from the pockets of the men who had been picked up in the raid, the tube of vaseline was the token of abjection itself, the kind of abjection that one takes the greatest care to conceal, but yet the token of a secret grace that was soon to save me from contempt." Abjection can no longer be confused with masochism here. Genet could not have said that the tube of vaseline was the token of masochism itself. There is no erotic thrill to be had in the smug derision of the police officer, who casts on Genet merely the cold, contemptuous eye of societal disapproval. Genet does not get any pleasure out of this disparaging treatment, but he does come to find in his very exposure to social condemnation an unexpected opportunity for surviving the annihilating force of conventional moral judgments.

"When I was locked up in a cell, and as soon as I was able to recover my spirits enough to rebound from the misery of my arrest, the image of that tube of vaseline never left me. The policemen had brandished it in front of me so as to flaunt their revenge, their hatred, their contempt. But lo and behold! that filthy, wretched object, whose purpose seemed to all the world" (meaning those muscular Spanish policemen, so morally sure of themselves) "to be utterly vile, became to me extremely precious." Unlike a lot of objects that Genet singles out for special tenderness, it was not surrounded in his eyes with an aureole of beauty: "it just sat there, on the table, a small dull grey leaden tube of vaseline, broken and livid," whose correspondence with all the common furnishings of the jail would have depressed him if it hadn't evoked for him "the preparation of so many secret joys," if it hadn't so often become "the condition of my happiness. . . . Lying on the table, it was a banner telling the invisible legions of my triumph over the police. I was in a holding cell. I knew that all night long my tube of vaseline would be exposed to the contempt of a group of strong, handsome, burly policemen: a reverse Adoration of the Magi. . . . Nonetheless, I was sure that this puny and most humble object would hold its own against them; by its mere presence it would be able to exasperate all the police in the world."[140]

The tube of vaseline and the vicissitudes of its public exposure perfectly convey the excruciating position of gay male sex in the heteronormative social scene. Genet's sexuality, including his homosexuality, his filthiness, his prostitution, his poverty, his youth, his subordination, his vulnerability, his anal receptivity, his sexual passivity, his emasculation—all that is helplessly, mercilessly displayed to public view by the tube of vaseline and made into an object of general contempt and derision. At the same time, the tube of vaseline is the visible sign of Genet's indestructible "secret joys," the material basis and outward symbol of an experience of intense pleasure and prohibited happiness that the straight world can scarcely imagine and will never know. The tube of vaseline is therefore not only "the token of abjection itself" but the token of gay sex itself in all its antisocial splendor: its filthiness, its disgracefulness, its thrills, its delirious risks and dangers, its defiance—its surprising strength as a source of instinctive, unconquerable pride and resistance. "I would have also liked to fight for it," Genet concludes.[141]

🌺 *This remarkable* portrait of abjection and its vicissi-tudes may well answer to the need Michael Warner and others have felt for a model of human behavior that can make sense of some gay men's continued sexual risk-tak-ing. For Genet's account of abjection produces a non-pathologizing discourse of gay male subjectivity that offers a way of understanding the motivation of marginalized individuals without representing their acts as either inten-tional or unintentional. And that is what the supposed conundrum of some gay men's practices of risk had seemed to call for. Which is why interpretative efforts that shifted the burden of explanation onto the psychoanalytic notion of the unconscious seemed so appealing. By con-trast, the opening pages of *The Thief's Journal* elaborate an aesthetic, rather than a psychoanalytic, approach to the workings of gay male subjectivity that similarly bypasses the problem of intentionality. As such, that approach can mediate between an inadequate understanding of risky sex as the result of deliberate choice (which it very rarely is) and an equally unsatisfactory view of risky sex as a com-plete accident (as the determinate outcome of factors entirely external to the subject, to which the subject itself does not contribute).

Because the gay transvaluation of abjection, as Genet describes it, does not express a conscious act of will any more than it registers an unwitting, passive reflex, Genet's account does not give rise to a model of agency that would resurrect the sovereign, universal human subject posited by the sort of liberal humanism that much modern philoso-phy and critical theory have tried so hard to dismantle. Sartre, to be sure, made Genet into an exemplar of human-ism, a witness to the irreducible fact of subjective agency and to the indestructible, inextinguishable, inescapable instinct of human freedom. That is why he emphasized Genet's resistance to social determination even at its most total and crushing; it is also why he foregrounded Genet's invention of the homosexual subject. And, indeed, throughout his writings, and especially in *The Thief's Jour-*

abjection includes disordered affect and reason.

licking the hand of the rapist.

...nal, Genet did insist on a voluntarist model of human agency, on his own unconquerable will, even celebrating "pride" as a "masculine virtue."[142] I have not hesitated to skip over those passages in Genet that support Sartre's humanist interpretation and that I consider both uninteresting in themselves and unhelpful for the project of elaborating a model of gay subjectivity without psychology. Genet is a highly uneven writer who does not always sustain his most original or radical insights. My argument leans on him, where necessary, but it does not aspire to represent his thinking as a whole.

The two brief passages from Genet that I have just discussed are noteworthy precisely because they do not lend themselves to Sartre's philosophical agenda. The humanist subject on which Sartre insists, with its sovereign properties of agency and freedom, is not on prominent display in them. In those two passages, at least, Genet does not present himself as pulling himself together, taking control of the situation, exercising agency, or making a choice. Nor does he see himself as a mere plaything of fate. Rather, something happens to him when he finds himself under extreme constraint, something whose exact "mechanism" he is "unable to describe" to us.

The process is mysterious: Genet doesn't act, nor is he merely acted on. The defiant response to abjection is not an innate human function, not the operation of a psychic law or structure, let alone the actualization of a property of the subject, such as agency. There's no guarantee that it will kick in—some people in Genet's situation might simply be crushed. In Genet's case, however, something happens. Fear turns into desire. Humiliation turns into defiance. Abjection discloses a secret grace that saves him from contempt.

magic.

Genet is not free to choose, nor is he compelled to act. Rather, he "slowly forced himself" to see his miserable condition as a necessity that he had willed on himself. It is not he who turns spit into roses. That is a result of the terrible pressure exerted on him by his love for Bulkaen as well as by his real and imagined social humiliations. Even if he has to mobilize considerable effort, the force of circumstance leaves Genet no option. The way of sainthood, as he says, is not one that can be avoided.

No wonder the strange reversals of abjection have something "miraculous" about them. Like pleasure, they happen at the very limit of the subject.[143] They do not arise from the fullness of intention, but neither do they take place in spite of it. Far from depending on or proceeding from the sovereignty of an already integrated subject, they illustrate how agency is constituted through the processes of subjectivation itself.[144] They leave room for what Berlant calls "lateral agency," by which she signifies that "agency can be an activity of maintenance, not making; fantasy, without grandiosity; sentience, without full intentionality; inconsistency, without shattering; embodying, alongside embodiment."[145] No one would ever accuse Genet of shunning grandiosity, but if it is true that agency never disappears from these two narratives of his, the kind of agency that does subsist in them is not agency in the sense of voluntarity or willful intention. Agency does not emerge here as the natural outcome of a developmental process, the unfolding of a psychic structure, a constitutive property of the subject. It is rather an effect of the play of social power: the unpredictable result of struggle.

VI

How might this tradition of queer reflection on the social-subjective dynamics of abjection offer a meaningful alternative to psychology or psychoanalysis for the purposes of HIV/AIDS prevention? Michael Warner had asked us to consider the possibility that abjection might be the unacknowledged but secret truth of the gay male subject—and that the reason some gay men engage in risky sex might be that the possibility of being infected with HIV connects up with the pleasure they take in being bad, in embracing society's judgment against them. The practice of sexual outlawry, including the rejection of safety and the courtship of risk, may therefore exert a monstrously powerful appeal on some gay men. Suppose, further, that Warner was correct. What conclusions should we draw from that diagnosis? Is abjection fatal, and do those gay men who get a thrill out of it need to be cured of their tendencies, for their own good? Or can we do other things with abjection besides die of it?

The answer hinges on how we understand abjection. If, on the one hand, abjection were to be pressed into a psychoanalytic idiom, forced to refer to something deep in the psychic structure of homosexuality that causes gay men to seek their own annihilation, that notion—however interesting or repugnant in itself—would be of little practical use for HIV/AIDS prevention, except insofar as it would explain why prevention efforts sometimes fail: they fail because they are futile, because gay men, unless saved by therapy, really (unconsciously) want to be killed. If, on the other hand, abjection names the social situation that forces us, in order to survive, to resist the crushing burden of shame, to glory in our exclusion from the scene of social belonging, to transcend (at least in our imagination) the humiliating realities of social existence, and to find in the secret history of our pleasures a source of personal and collective triumph over the forces that would destroy us, then abjection would seem to have some life-enhancing uses. Abjection is not the problem, in other words, but the solution. Or, at least, it is not *just* a problem, but also a possible solution. On this latter *queer* interpretation, abjection would not represent a very deep or dark secret, of the sort that only psychoanalysis can reveal, but an observable social phenomenon, whose implications for HIV/AIDS prevention remain to be carefully thought out. After all, the genius of gay sex—and not only *gay* sex—lies precisely in its ability to transmute otherwise unpleasant experiences of social degradation into experiences of pleasure. That indeed is one of the good things about sex, one of the things sex is good for, and one of the things people cherish about it.

The antisocial thrill of abjection may be powerful enough to tempt gay men (and other despised social groups) to risk becoming infected with HIV, then, but it is not necessarily destructive. Abjection does not specifically manifest a death wish or death drive, a lack of self-respect, a pleasure in suffering, or a belief that one does not deserve to survive.[146] Nor, on the contrary, does it simply express a sense of pride in one's pleasure and in one's right to have it, a sense of pride sufficiently strong to enable one to afford and to withstand the humiliations that are pleasure's price—or even, sometimes, pleasure's necessary precondition.[147] Rather, abjection describes a particular attitude to both suffering and pleasure, to both shame and pride, to both humility and grandiosity, by which those terms can be brought into relation. It is an experiment with the limits of both destruction and survival, social isolation and social solidarity, domination and transcendence. Instead of worrying about the appeal of abjection to gay men, then, and wondering what to do about it, what we really should be doing is trying to think concretely about how to mobilize the transformative power of abjection, how to make it work for us.

🌹 *That may not* be as easy as it sounds. It certainly should not imply that abjection can simply be instrumentalized at will—transformed into a science, a politics, or some kind of New Age therapy. (Feeling self-destructive lately? Try some abjection. A little dose will do you.) For the purposes of HIV/AIDS activism, abjection clearly cuts both ways. It provides a defense against the social stigma of HIV infection, even as it also complicates the work of HIV/AIDS prevention.

For example, it may prove vital for those infected with HIV not to mystify the virus, not to turn it in their imaginations into a representation of pure evil. They may find it necessary, transformative, even lifesaving to be able to capitalize on their status as pariahs—and to think about their own bodies not just as bearers of contagion, not only as poisoned or ruined, but also as sparkling with viral light, as harbingers of a new ecology, as an evolutionary stage in a process of mutation whereby humans will someday live with HIV the way we now live with the common cold, and as putting to shame with their beauty and strangeness the legions of sex-hating neighbors, finger-shaking doctors, moralizing preachers, judgmental gay pundits, and outraged prevention activists.[148] "I accidentally saw myself at that moment in a mirror," writes Hervé Guibert in his fictionalized AIDS memoir, *To the Friend Who Did Not Save My Life*, describing a routine visit to a clinic, where a medical technician is in the process of drawing a sample of his blood, "and I found myself extraordinarily beautiful, although I had not seen anything more than a skeleton for several months."[149] Guibert realizes that he has to love this body of his which HIV has transformed.

Like Bulkaen, who (at least in Genet's imagined, aestheticized version of him) transmuted acts of violence into rites of love, Guibert experiences a sudden, spontaneous illumination. Both men's altered perceptions come to them unwilled. They are not deliberately worked up for the occasion, not the result of positive thinking, hard-won self-acceptance, or healthy self-love. Rather, they reflect involuntarily the intense pressure of savage social stigma and crushing material need. HIV-positive gay men who come to embrace their outcast status, who actually feel *liberated* by social rejection, and who come to see the virus as a flower no less than as a dangerous microbe—who can imagine their infected selves, in other words, both as pelted by spit and showered with roses, all at the same time—they enact a kind of abjection that may have similarly life-enhancing uses.

By way of a particularly telling example, Kane Race considers the case of the late Scott O'Hara—gay porn star, writer, activist, and self-proclaimed inventor of an ethic of "barebacking." O'Hara's own memoir, which Race quotes at length, testifies to the sense of exaltation that O'Hara felt in embracing and reversing the abjection attached to HIV infection. As O'Hara himself acknowledged, he became "notorious" in the mid-1990s for his "positions on HIV," including the view that "in my life, AIDS has been an undeniable blessing. It woke me up to what was important; it let me know that NOW was the time to do it."

O'Hara's explanation of the advantages he derived from being infected emphasized the way his HIV-positive status consolidated a long-standing attitude of social defiance, connected no doubt with the abjection of homosexuality itself.

And—this is the part that upsets people—it also gives me the freedom to behave "irresponsibly." I look at the HIV-negative people around me, and I pity them. They live their lives in constant fear of infection: mustn't do this, mustn't do that, mustn't take risks. They can't see past that simple "avoidance of infection," which has come to be their ultimate goal. . . . My life is so much more carefree than theirs, so much more "considered," that I shake my head and count myself lucky to have been infected. Risk taking is the essence of life, and people who spend their entire lives trying to eliminate risk from their lives are . . . well, they're not my kind of people. I know a couple of people who have self-consciously made the decision to serocon-vert; I admire them tremendously, because it takes a consider-able amount of self-confidence and self-knowledge to make a decision that flies in the face of every medical and journalistic opinion in the world.[150]

Race makes it clear that O'Hara's promotion of bareback-ing did not imply any casualness about the possibility of infecting HIV-negative men. On the contrary, O'Hara was careful not to put his HIV-negative partners at risk and made an effort to have unprotected anal sex only with men who were or who might be plausibly construed to be HIV-positive. He was famous for having the sign *HIV+* tattooed on his shoulder back in 1994, so that no one who had unprotected sex with him could mistake the nature of the risk involved—beyond which the choice was up to them.

For O'Hara, then, behaving "'irresponsibly'" meant defying the safe-sex rule of "use a condom every time." He put the word "irresponsibly" in quotation marks in his text to indicate that he was citing respectable society's (includ-ing respectable gay society's) definition: it was *their* notion of responsibility he was defying. And defying that restric-tive, moralizing notion of responsibility was entirely con-sistent with adhering to his own quite rigorous ethic of care for others. He admired those possessed of the assur-ance needed to fly in the face of authority and public opin-ion, and his transvaluation of the meaning of being infected with HIV demonstrated the sense of freedom afforded by "the rejection of normal life." O'Hara clearly found liberation in abjection. Moreover, abjection led him to forge new sexual communities and cultures among the outcast, the shamed, the excluded. To the extent that he can be counted, for that reason, as a pioneer of "serosort-ing," as Race argues, his defiance actually conduced to the invention of more adaptive and innovative practices of safety than the outmoded condom etiquette that he took such pleasure in defying.

As O'Hara's commendation of those who deliberately choose to seroconvert also indicates, however, abjection may be less useful for getting HIV-negative gay men to minimize their risks of infection. To the extent that it is associated with an impulse in gay men to play out to the limit the logic of social exclusion and denigration, to be the sexual outlaws that society has made of us,[151] abjection may be the reason why some gay men cherish risky sex and even desire infection, as Warner also implied. And if we conceive of abjection as a collective response to social humiliation, rather than as an individual pathology, it may even be possible to think of HIV infection among gay men as a scary but inspired expression of antisocial solidarity with their sick or dead comrades in ignominy.[152] Just as Genet wished to save Bulkaen from his isolation and to join him in the very depths of his shame, some HIV-negative men might play with risk as a way of making common cause with the HIV-positive men they love. If Genet had been born in the same year as O'Hara, his quest for sainthood would surely have inspired him to get himself infected with HIV.

Or not. Genet turns out to have been a survivor *par excellence.* He somehow got through reformatory and prison, misery and destitution, and the generally appalling conditions of his early life, not to mention the Nazi occupation of France (he escaped being deported by the skin of his teeth—and by the timely intervention of well-placed, influential friends). He was an orphan, a juvenile delinquent, a deserter, a mental case, and, all his life, a thief. (A warning to those who would take Genet to be representative of a privileged, white, gay male élite: there is virtually no one in U.S. academe who can claim to have come from a more humble, a more deprived background than Genet, who was in and out of prison throughout the first half of his life, living on the street and turning tricks in order to

Self-/
destruction!

Creation!

survive, and whose longing for high cultural achievement was in exact proportion to the social degradation of his origins.) Genet had multiple opportunities to translate his taste for abjection into literal self-destruction, but he does not seem to have been in any particular hurry to take them. He ran considerable risks, yet in the end he did not get himself killed, or seriously harmed. He made money, enjoyed forty years of literary celebrity, and lived to the age of seventy-five.

There are, then, other possibilities. Abjection might be compatible with a certain degree of self-defense. It might express itself in love and camaraderie with other abject individuals. Abjection could make HIV-negative gay men defiant, fiercely protective of their queer pleasures, determined to have all the filthy gay sex they want without having to pay the fatal price for it that our society would prefer to exact from them. In the case of HIV-positive men, abjection may be responsible for some of the "breed me" fantasy scenarios, in which positive guys pretend to be negative guys seeking positive partners to infect them with HIV, using the fiction of HIV-transmission to ramp up the transgressive intensity of the encounter, to heighten the thrill of submission, to attract kinky tops, and to endow the relative banality of seroconcordant sex with novelty and excitement.[153] Abjection might in these ways fuel the drive to prevention, not subvert it.

Here is another possible scenario. Because HIV infection is still surrounded by shame in gay communities, there is understandable pressure to conceal it, to make the human face of infection disappear from sight, and to deny the extent of the epidemic, so as to prevent it from obstructing the continuing pursuit of sexual pleasure. The shame that attaches to being infected with HIV is therefore very dangerous: it gets in the way of self-disclosure, obscures the threats to their health that gay men face in their sexual activities, and encourages panic and avoidance. In these ways it may increase the risks of HIV transmission.[154] But what happens when HIV is deprived of its terror, when its shame-inducing power is accepted, even embraced—when, as Brent Armendinger puts it, elaborating on Genet's image, "roses are allowed to fall on an object, when spit is not merely thrown? What role does fear play in the velocity of risk and what changes occur when roses dissolve this fear?"[155] Genet does not mistake spit for roses, after all: he knows (or he imagines) he is being spit on, but—in his determination to survive and to be free—he interprets the gesture as an act of love. Would such an attitude of defiance, which does not deny the horror of suffering but both mobilizes and transcends the shame of it, enable HIV infection to become less disavowed and more accepted, more visible—in a word, more real—in communities of gay men? Might it thereby become more preventable?

🌸 *Abjection may not* exactly lend itself to pro-gay propaganda, to being operationalized as public health policy, but it could still have an important role to play in HIV/AIDS prevention. Notable in this connection is queer culture's long track record of making productive use of abjection. The mere title of Bruce LaBruce's legendary 1990 zine, *Dumb Bitch Deserves to Die,* speaks eloquently to the ingenuity of queer culture in converting the abjection inflicted by HIV/AIDS into a potent resource for social defiance. An even better example would be the brilliant (and somewhat longer-lived) San Francisco zine for HIV-positive gay men, *Diseased Pariah News,* founded by Tom Shearer and Beowulf Thorne, which also began publication in 1990 and tried to devise fresh methods for putting across to gay men the urgency of HIV prevention (Scott O'Hara contributed an eight-part serial to it, at once cautionary and tongue-in-cheek, called "How I Got AIDS"). The trick is to come up with a non-pathologizing account of abjection, and that means, in the case of gay male abjection, a collective, social, non-psychoanalytic account of it. For only a non-psychoanalytic account of abjection can deal with *the social specificity of abjection's appeal to gay men* without attributing to gay men as a group a defective psychic condition.

Gregory Tomso has astutely underscored this point. "If we take Freud's theory of the death drive seriously, and acknowledge a general desire for death underlying all of human behavior, there is still reason to be suspicious of the particular linking of barebacking and bug chasing with a desire for death. Acknowledging a general human tendency toward self-destruction is not the same as endorsing the homophobic, rhetorical linkage of particular sexual acts (unprotected anal sex) by particular people (gay men) with a desire for particular acts of death (suicide and murder)."[156] In other words, a universal drive, even if one existed, could never explain the distinctive and distinguishing collective behavior of a specific social subgroup, defined by particular social vicissitudes.[157] Otherwise, psychoanalysis turns into sociology, and sociology does not support such generalizations in any case: as Barry Adam and his colleagues report, on the basis of extensive interview data, "It must be stressed, against the panic icons of barebackers and bug-chasers circulating in the press and in popular discourse, that none of these practices nor the moral reasoning associated with them overtly intend HIV transmission to happen."[158]

If, however, we think of abjection not as the symptom of an unconscious drive to self-annihilation, but as *a strategic response to a specific social predicament*—as a socially constituted affect that can intensify the determination to survive, can conduce to sexual inventiveness, and can lead to the creation of various devices for extracting heightened pleasure, and even love, from experiences of pain, fear, rejection, humiliation, contempt, shame, brutality, disgust, or condemnation—then we have no reason to believe that abjection is more particularly responsible for gay men's willingness to have risky sex than any of the other factors that I have enumerated, or that it puts gay men at a particularly heightened risk of contracting HIV, or that it makes gay men particularly impervious to HIV/AIDS education. And we don't need psychoanalysts to help us deal with it. We need social theorists and activists like Michael Warner and Douglas Crimp to help us reflect on its power and perils. It is Crimp himself who once argued, after all, that it was our very perversity that would save us from HIV/AIDS, by teaching us how to invent, in the midst of crisis, new modalities of pleasure.[159] Genet's example would seem to back up that claim.

🌹 *Warner's essay* itself can be taken as illustrative of it as well. For not only does it *relate* the story of Warner's abjection, by narrating his acts of unsafe sex: it also *enacts* his abjection. I am referring to Warner's decision to write and publish that essay of his in a mass-circulation weekly newspaper in his own hometown. It can't very well have been easy for a prominent gay intellectual, commentator, and academic to sacrifice his privacy and to come out in the pages of the *Village Voice* as a sex criminal (for that is how those who fuck without condoms were coming to be viewed by the nascent culture of safer sex at the time), or as someone who had lost control of his own sex life and was animated by mental processes akin to what he himself called "impulse shoplifting" (33). Nor can it have been easy for any politically savvy member of the gay community, such as Warner, to expose the workings of his and other gay men's subjectivity to public scrutiny in the context of a society and a media culture that for years had been trafficking endlessly and dangerously in sensationalistic images of gay men's demented sexual extremism.

But it also can't have been all that hard for Warner to do what he did, because any non-normative sexual subject who has ever had to come out of the closet cannot fail to have experienced something of the paradox of abjection: the more people despise you, the less you owe them, and the freer and more powerful you are. The contempt in which you are held, and the isolation it imposes, also open up rare but precious opportunities for love and solidarity among the outcast. The social drama of abjection (a tradi-

ethnocentric
genealogical inquiry

tion of secular erotic martyrdom distinctive to modernism that reaches back to Rousseau and Baudelaire) consists in its amplification of the individual's importance—in the way it endows him with an inverted glamour, an antisocial prestige. Contempt is the price of publicity, the trade-off for personal transfiguration. Abjection registers the paradox of social violence, which both degrades and glorifies.

Gay men have long been inured to that sort of thing. It is no wonder that Warner could muster the resolve needed to occupy the same sort of social space as Genet's tube of vaseline—to risk offering himself up to derision, contempt, and normalizing judgments, and to make himself an occasion for the smug moralism and righteous self-congratulation of those (straight or gay) people who pride themselves on being normal.

If we hesitate to give Warner great moral credit for his courageous choice, if we are reluctant to view him in consequence of it as a saint, that may say less about our own lack of generosity than it does about our suspicion that Warner may also have gotten a kick out of composing that remarkable article. Did he not get off on making a spectacle of himself? Does his whole text not quiver with the excitement of writing it? His courage, though undeniable, seems less an expression of bravery than of bravado. But that, of course, is entirely consistent with the point I am making here about the uses of abjection. It is precisely because Warner—in risking his reputation by talking about his practices of risk—could get a heady thrill out of his mortifying self-exposure, that the very writing and publication of his essay can qualify as an illustration of, and a lesson in, the workings of abjection that Genet so vividly and powerfully portrayed. It was Warner's queer ability to find both pleasure and defiance in the social humiliation he knew he would incur by publishing his article that also gave him the strength and the drive to produce it. Warner thereby demonstrated the political uses of abjection. By his very example he showed how abjection can work not only to put gay subjects at risk but also to enable them to confront and survive those risks—and, just maybe, to overcome them.

Ultimately, then, the value of abjection may lie in its promotion of self-abandonment. The most striking examples of abjection I have considered are dramatic or heroic, but Warner's own practice suggests that abjection may also consist in simply *losing yourself* as an all-important project, putting other things ahead of your ego. Perhaps in this way abjection can help to de-dramatize the practice of sexual risk, something we need particularly to do in the context of the current panic over barebacking. It is here that Lauren Berlant's approach to obesity may offer a useful parallel, insofar as it highlights practices of self-interruption and self-abandonment that make no claim to heroic agency, even as they also refuse to lapse into total surrender. "In the model I am articulating here, the body and a life are not only projects but also sites of episodic intermission from personality, of inhabiting agency differently in small vacations from the will itself, which is so often spent from the pressures of coordinating one's pacing with the pace of the working day, including times of preparation and recovery from it. These pleasures can be seen as interrupting the liberal and capitalist subject called to consciousness, intentionality, and effective will."[160]

Modern postindustrial societies produce social conditions that seem to foster in their citizens a yearning for escape, exemption, "small vacations from the will itself," self-loss, transcendence. Abjection offers one such opportunity; the voluntary pursuit of risk offers another; pleasure (whether it involves sex, eating, or shopping) holds out a third. It is because risky sex manages to conjoin and condense all three of those modes of wished-for transcendence—abjection, risk, and pleasure—that it remains both so seductive and so unmanageable. Whether we succeed in devising ways to make the appeal of abjection conduce to forms of self-loss that enhance our lives and communities will depend, in the end, on our mutual understanding and our political determination.

❧ *Let me make* it very clear that I am not suggesting we posit "abjection" as the secret truth of gay male subjectivity. Nor do I want to offer a new definition of gay male subjectivity grounded in the social vicissitudes of abjection, let alone to substitute abjection for the death drive as the privileged explanation for gay men's sexual risk-taking. Michael Warner did look to abjection for explanatory insight, and I find his hypothesis plausible, but it is not my purpose to prove it to be true. Even the most rudimentary account of gay male subjectivity, in order to be minimally satisfying, would have to allow room for very many other sorts of distinctive gay affect besides abjection alone. I have wanted to linger over Warner's claim, without taking a position on its correctness, in order to develop my main argument, which is that there exist countertraditions of reflection on queer subjectivity that are worthy of serious consideration and that offer meaningful alternatives to psychology and psychoanalysis.

My point is not that psychoanalysis is intrinsically hostile to queers or unadapted to a just appreciation and analysis of queer eroticism. That has yet to be established; if true, it would require a lengthy separate demonstration. My intent has not been to disqualify psychoanalysis in all its forms, but to put us on guard against a stealth "return of the normal" within psychoanalytic criticism. For that purpose, I have not had to adduce any additional evidence beyond the particular texts I have cited here. Those texts symptomatize a more general tendency, however, to which I have wished to call attention: namely, the frequency with which even the most ostensibly radical, anti-normative psychoanalytic projects rehabilitate—sometimes unwittingly, and despite the explicit denials of their authors—normalizing judgments in the realm of sex, sexuality, and gender. Not all versions of psychoanalysis pathologize deviations from the norm to the same extent, but the task of apportioning various degrees of blame or legitimacy to psychoanalysis, justifying it, and distinguishing better from worse versions of it is not one that falls to me. I am

happy to let psychoanalytic critics deal with those challenges themselves. Once the pitfalls of psychoanalytic
approaches have been located and described, it will be up
to those who wish to continue to practice psychoanalytic
criticism to figure out how to avoid them.

My aim, then, is not to refute psychoanalytic doctrine
or to show that psychoanalysis is irredeemably heterosex-
ist, but simply to explain why I believe psychoanalysis
should not be the only critical show in homo-town. We
should license ourselves at least to contemplate the possibility of exploring other approaches to understanding the
human subject, even less rigorous or theoretically evolved
approaches to understanding the human subject, without
necessarily feeling that we are committing a thought-
crime. And, in particular, we may find it valuable to imagine alternate, non-normalizing methods of looking into
the workings of gay male subjectivity.

If I have been concerned so persistently with abjection,
that is because it figured centrally in the effort Michael
Warner made to produce a non-pathologizing account of
why some gay men have risky sex. I have treated abjection,
in other words, not as an essential gay male experience but
as a found object. My goal has been to show that, when-
ever talk about sex and risk turns to abjection, as it does in
Warner's essay, we can move the conversation in a non-
psychoanalytic direction by mobilizing existing resources
of queer thought. We need only follow the lines of interpretation already implicit in Warner's article but not fully
laid out there.

And if we can do that with abjection, we can also do it
with other psychologically or psychoanalytically freighted
concepts.

I do think abjection has much to recommend it as a way
of thinking about the social constitution of gay male subjectivity. But I don't wish to claim that what Jean Genet
wrote in a different context sixty years ago provides the key
to understanding the inner logic of gay men's sexual
behavior in the present. Nor do I intend to install abjec-

tion in place of psychology or psychoanalysis as the foundation for a new science of the gay subject. The significance of abjection in this context lies in the way it points to the existence and availability of alternative approaches—social approaches, queer approaches—to the project of describing the subjective life of homosexuality.

I do believe Warner was right to insist on the need to incorporate questions of queer affect or subjectivity into HIV/AIDS prevention strategies. His effort should inspire us to advance that project, while cautioning us against rushing to conceptualize the inner life of male homosexuality in psychoanalytic terms, especially since it turns out that viable queer alternatives are available. It is possible to acknowledge the lure of abjection to gay men without imputing to us a deep desire to be annihilated—or picturing us as possessed, like the doomed race in the 1956 sci-fi movie classic *Forbidden Planet,* by "monsters from the Id." And that should make it easier to talk openly among ourselves about the uses of surrender and abasement, about our complex relations to social and sexual humiliation, and about our occasional courtship of risk, because now we won't have to worry that such talk will come across as punitive or pathologizing.

More important, without the possibility of falling back on commonplaces of psychoanalytic theory for explanatory insight, we won't be able to dodge the hard, specific questions about why some of us, *here, now,* take risks in our sexual practices. Nor will we be able to ignore so easily all the specific, contingent, determining historical and social factors, such as the woeful lack in the United States of a national HIV/AIDS prevention strategy or of a community standard and authorized discourse of HIV/AIDS *risk reduction,* and the particular, catastrophic consequences of the unrealistic, panicky, and outdated strategy of *risk elimination.* And then perhaps we may be able to work out some communal agreements about how to integrate our volatile relationship to risk into workable

HIV/AIDS risk reduction practices. Some of that, indeed, seems already to be happening, at a grassroots level.[161]

The real challenge of HIV/AIDS prevention, in short, would seem to demand *not* a psychoanalytic effort to identify and disclose our deepest drives, but the collective intelligence to outsmart a virus and the courage to surmount our shame about the abject pleasures we actually enjoy. The inhibition we need to overcome, in other words, is not psychical but social. Which is why Warner decided to break social taboos and publish that article of his in the first place.

myth

Collective enlightenment = collective HIV infection

VII

"*How can we* successfully combat AIDS without understanding the appeal of sexual self-immolation and the full range of defensive reactions to that appeal?" That seems to me to be the practical challenge that Michael Warner's example leaves us with. It is a question of halting the epidemic by social means without having to derive prevention initiatives from dubious speculations about the human psyche. The formulation I have just quoted, however, is not a summons to think either non-psychoanalytically or practically about how to stop AIDS. The question is not Michael Warner's but Tim Dean's, and, to his discredit, it is not a practical question but a rhetorical one, designed to impugn any attempt at HIV/AIDS prevention that is not psychoanalytically informed. "How [on earth]," Dean asks, neither desiring nor expecting an answer, "can we successfully combat AIDS without understanding the appeal of sexual self-immolation and the full range of defensive reactions to that appeal?"[162] The urgent questions, it seems to me, are actually the opposite. Not only how, specifically, can we combat the HIV/AIDS epidemic *without* treating it as a symptom of an alleged death drive, a death drive that somehow ends up becoming the peculiar property of gay men and people living with HIV/AIDS, but also how can a prevention strategy that does focus on "the appeal of sexual self-immolation" ever produce anything useful by way of an HIV/AIDS education initiative?

In all the writing I know that insists on our reckoning with the death drive as the only realistic way to confront the deep causes of HIV transmission, I cannot think of *a single concrete or practical proposal* for stopping the epi-

demic that has been put forward on that basis. The usefulness of the death drive in fact would appear to be the
reverse of what its proponents typically claim. Far from
being what is most necessary for gay men to take into
account in order to halt the spread of HIV/AIDS, it would
seem that HIV/AIDS has become what is most necessary
for psychoanalytic critics to take into account nowadays in
order to craft a plausible and persuasive theory of the death
drive. It is not prevention activists who need the death
drive in order to stop the epidemic: it is psychoanalytic
theorists who need the epidemic in order to make us
believe once again in the death drive.

All the more reason, then, to resist them.

To be sure, my own argument might be vulnerable to
an identical critique. Have I put forward a single concrete
or practical proposal for stopping the HIV/AIDS epidemic
on the basis of the anti-psychological approach that I have
been lobbying for? I have invoked some practical examples
of the uses of abjection for queer survival. And I have indicated how defying social condemnation might actually
serve the cause of HIV/AIDS prevention. But I have deliberately refrained from proposing a specific program of
action, since it is not in the nature of effective social interventions to be directly deducible from theoretical paradigms. And I have not wanted to preempt practical thinking about how to stop the spread of HIV, which must be
done within the context of particular social situations and
requires both concrete social analysis and considerable
practical imagination.[163] I do not presume to instruct
activists on the best strategies of prevention.

The usefulness of my undertaking, as I see it, consists
specifically in debunking and clearing away an accumulation of psychological and psychoanalytic theories that
impede concrete, practical interventions or, even worse,
imply that such interventions are doomed to failure.
Rather than try to substitute one theory for another, I have
tried to resist presenting the challenge of prevention as a
theoretical one, except insofar as it has been unnecessarily

complicated by the multiplication of bogus theories about gay men's defective psychology—and therefore requires a theoretical response. Instead of coming up with a new and better theory, one allegedly able to generate new prevention initiatives, I have tried to produce *a critical anti-theory* that opens up the possibility of addressing the question of sex and risk in practical terms uncontaminated by normative thinking about gay men's psychology. That has been the purpose behind my search for alternative, non-disciplinary models of gay male subjectivity.

Foucault was right, I believe, to go to considerable lengths in order to avoid grounding the study of gay sexuality in an analysis of the gay subject. And it is understandable that many queer theorists should have followed his lead by trying to close off all access to the category of the psychic and by approaching gay subjectivity as an effect of a political technology.[164] But is every inquiry into the distinctive features of gay male subjectivity destined to produce homophobic results? Do good politics, *safe* politics, require us to closet the subjective life of male homosexuality?

I have tried to indicate here that it is possible, by evading the claims of psychology and psychoanalysis to be the master sciences of the subject, to give an account of gay male subjectivity that is neither individualizing nor psychically empty, neither normalizing nor politically defensive. Here is where the tradition of representing gay male subjectivity in terms of abjection comes in handy. It offers an approach that does not neglect the affective dimensions of gay life but represents them in an existential idiom that makes reference to the particular vicissitudes of gay men's social being and resists being translated immediately into the language of pathology. It addresses the same object intended by psychological science—namely, the human subject—but it apprehends that object by a variety of queer means (by which I mean both *non-standard* means and *homosexually inflected* means). In that way, it exemplifies an alternative to a science of individually psychologized subjectivity. And it shifts the definition of subjectivity itself.

🌸 *When compared* to the languages of social and medical science, the rhetoric of religious and erotic martyrdom that goes by the name of abjection would seem to be fatally flawed: vaporous, unspecific, lacking in precision and the power of rigorous description. But that is exactly what makes it useful. In an age when we overvalue method, endowing conventional academic and social scientific procedure with a sheen of objectivity, these flaws, this weakness, and the related lack of an associated dogma or elaborate theory, can qualify as a strength. It reminds us of what we do not know.

Abjection, as it emerges from the tradition I have described, is a manifestly rhetorical figure. It does not pretend to be scientific. It cannot be mistaken for an authoritative discourse. Abjection remains a phenomenological description, and so it does not make the same claim on our literal belief as a would-be science does. Because it derives from the archaic and discredited language of an outmoded, fairy-tale brand of religiosity, it is in no danger of producing truth. Its power depends only on its usefulness, its degree of fit with what we feel, its aptitude for capturing the quality of lived experience. And so abjection cannot lend itself easily to the purposes of a normalizing discourse, whose authority is legitimated by its access to truth. With abjection, we cannot fool ourselves: we know we are dealing with a metaphor for our feelings, not with our feelings themselves. Better, then, a gothic language of abjection or martyrdom—a set of figural linguistic gestures whose outlandish Catholic kitsch prevents anyone from taking them literally—than the presumptively objective, theoretically elaborated, scientific languages of psychology and psychoanalysis, with all their glittering jargons and, far worse, their terrifying institutional, social, and political authority.

Abjection, at least, is not a diagnosis. You won't find it in the *DSM*. No one will be locked up or medicated on account of it.

Fortunately, the two idioms I have been playing off each other—religious spirituality and psychoanalysis—are not the only options, the only discourses that offer ways to understand the human subject. There are others that yield distinct models of subjectivity, and still others that can be composed by hybridizing them. Although some of the privileged terms in my analysis, such as shame, may seem to be psychological, and although some of the questions about human motivation under consideration here traditionally fall within the branch of philosophy that is sometimes called "moral psychology," I have consistently looked to sources other than psychology for my concepts. The languages of moral sentiments, social vicissitudes, stigma (branding), exclusion, and abjection come from alternative intellectual worlds. I admit that I have not hesitated to combine different analytical languages as I have seen fit, nor have I inscribed my own discourse within a single, coherent intellectual tradition.

But I have not been trying to invent a counter-science of the human subject. Rather, I have been trying to resist the self-evidence of the psychologized subject in order to leave open the possibility for other ways of thinking about and representing human affective life. I have wanted to champion, against the intellectual monoculture of psychology, a plurality of unsystematic approaches, largely sociological and aesthetic in inspiration, which are not the exclusive property of any particular discipline. My ultimate aim is not only to reconsider the gay male subject, but the subject as such. My working assumption has been that the human subject is part of the larger field of social power without however being reducible to it.[165] Current controversies over some gay men's practices of risky sex and the question of gay male subjectivity, if they do nothing else, certainly dramatize the subject's implication in cross-cutting systems of power.

I acknowledge that the queer account of abjection I have tried to resuscitate here is strangely upbeat and sentimental. A feel-good version of abjection: what could be more alien to the spirit of Genet?[166] The value of Genet for current queer critique has lain in his refusal of a normative ethics, and yet my account has come very close to finding in a couple of passages from his work the inspiration for an ethical vision. But I have also tried to stop just short of that tipping-point, short of turning abjection into either an ethics or a politics. At least, I have avoided making abjection into a political rallying-cry. The political uses of abjection have to do, after all, with the ways that abjection is *not* politics, with its resistance to anything so positive, healthy, earnest, or virtuous as a proper political program. If abjection could be transformed into such a program, it would lose its political usefulness, which consists in refusing the normativity of politics. But that doesn't mean abjection is politically vacuous either. My aim here has been to bring out the dimension of abjection that can contribute to politics—while stopping just short of turning it into politics, so as to preserve the apolitical dimension of abjection in which its political utility consists.

❧ *Surveying the* discursive scene of modern psychobabble in 1982, with its constant talk of "getting back to oneself, freeing oneself, being oneself, being authentic," Michel Foucault did not find that "we have anything to be proud of in our current undertakings to reconstitute an ethics of the self." And yet, he went on, "it may be an urgent, fundamental, and politically indispensable task, if it is true after all that there is no other point of resistance to political power, neither first nor last, than in the relation of oneself to oneself."[167] The difficult, vexed attitude to pleasure and danger, to sex and risk, on the part of many gay men in the age of HIV/AIDS provides an unexpected and pointed illustration of Foucault's claim. For it is precisely in the relation of the self to itself that gay men may have to look for a source of resistance to political power.

After all, the most intimate details of gay men's personal lives and sexual practices have been, for some time now, the target of relentless inquiry by an army of socially accredited experts in public health, epidemiology, sociology, psychology, and medicine, who claim to know with some assurance what it is that gay men want—and who prescribe to gay men, on that basis, an extensive set of moral, legal, and hygienic responsibilities. Their authoritative pronouncements, along with all the other discourses surrounding the practice and management of the gay self, place contemporary gay subjects under many kinds of personal, political, epistemological, analytical, and ethical pressure. In this situation of confusion, uncertainty, and stress, the relation of oneself to oneself turns out to be a particularly intense site of struggle. And so what Foucault designated by "an ethics of the self" is for many gay men not just some fashionable academic catchphrase or obscure tenet of postmodern theory, but a central problem, a collective project, even an urgent political necessity.

It is striking that many of the terms which feature in Foucault's own anti-psychological hermeneutics of the subject recur in Genet's queer language of abjection. Both writers speak, for example, of "ascesis" and "spiritual exercises."[168] Is it an accident, a coincidence, or a case of direct literary inheritance that Foucault and Genet, both gay writers, each of them confronting in his own way the burdens of psycho-normative culture, found in these outmoded vocabularies of spirituality an alternative, non-disciplinary model of subjectivity?

What HIV/AIDS prevention requires, in any case, is precisely such a non-disciplinary model of subjectivity. That has been the central thesis of my argument throughout the sometimes meandering course of this lengthy essay. In order to promote that non-disciplinary model of subjectivity, we will ultimately need to take abjection and spirituality out of the realm of miracle and transcendence—and return them to the vicissitudes of social existence. Both Genet and Foucault give us hints about how to do that.

The kind of work of the self on the self that Foucault himself defined as spirituality is not opposed to, but actually consists in, an ongoing labor of analysis, understanding, political sensitivity and responsiveness, communication, and community. Each one of Genet's scenes of martyrdom is a lyrical moment, a perfect aria without ensuing narrative, a one-act drama with no sequel. But perfect and complete as each one of them is, it does not stand alone. It is repeated. There is a sequence of such perfect moments. These "miracles of horror," as Sartre called them, are what Genet's writing, at its best, specializes in. They necessarily take place in time and history. Abjection as a social practice is therefore not a one-night stand. Or, rather, if it is a one-night stand, it is one of a series. Each new miracle has a history because there has been a miracle before it: this ongoingness, this daily relation of self to self, this continual return to time, this enduring engagement with the practical challenges of life are all part of each event. And it is in such a return to time, such an engagement with life, that abjection comes into contact with politics.

It may prove crucial at certain moments for minoritized subjects to be able to suspend time and history, to escape from them. But if it is to succeed, HIV/AIDS prevention, like abjection, requires repetition. It needs a miracle every day. Repetition is where miracle and history meet, and it is where, if anywhere, safe sex becomes habitual. When the miraculous becomes habitual, becomes historical, it can do the work of politics.[169]

Foucault speculated that "power relations / governmentality / the government of the self and of others / the relationship of self to self—all this constitutes a chain, a thread." He therefore tended to "think it is in connection with these notions that we should be able to link up the question of politics and the question of ethics."[170] If they suggest nothing else, the long series of interlocking arguments and analyses presented here indicate, I hope, how urgently we need more astute strategies and practical solutions for connecting politics and ethics. One crucial component of such a solution, of such a strategy, is a new working model of gay male subjectivity, a non-disciplinary model of gay subjectivity. Only such a non-disciplinary model of gay subjectivity—that is, a subjectivity which is not a subjectivity of risk, an object of social hygiene, or a target of therapeutic intervention—can provide the basis for the imaginative, resourceful, non-psychological, and non-moralistic strategy that HIV/AIDS prevention requires, both in the realm of personal practice and in the realm of public policy.

Then gay subjectivity, far from having to be bracketed, denied, suppressed, or closeted, can do what it has often done. It can impel political resistance.

Notes

1. See Mark Merlis, *American Studies* (1994; New York: Penguin, 1996) and *An Arrow's Flight* (New York: St. Martin's, 1998), for some astute novelistic arguments to the effect that gay men ultimately seek not sex but love and acceptance, specifically from other men, and that what we desire most of all is to be enfolded in the easy-going masculine erotics of straight male culture.

The view that HIV/AIDS prevention efforts need to reckon with a gay male death drive is rehearsed and criticized below, in section IV of this essay.

For an elaboration and qualification of my claim about queer studies, see my essay "Homosexuality's Closet," *Michigan Quarterly Review* 41.1 (Winter 2002): 21–54. It may be worth noting that the most ambitious and heroic recent efforts to capture gay male subjectivity have come from outside mainstream queer theory: Neil Bartlett, *Who Was That Man? A Present for Mr Oscar Wilde* (London: Serpent's Tail, 1988); David Nimmons, *The Soul Beneath the Skin: The Unseen Hearts and Habits of Gay Men* (New York: St. Martin's, 2002); and Will Fellows, *A Passion to Preserve: Gay Men as Keepers of Culture* (Madison: University of Wisconsin Press, 2004). There are, of course, some distinguished exceptions to this generalization: principally, D. A. Miller, *Place for Us [Essay on the Broadway Musical]* (Cambridge: Harvard University Press, 1998). See also (in alphabetical order) Teresa de Lauretis, *The Practice of Love: Lesbian Sexuality and Perverse Desire* (Bloomington: Indiana University Press, 1994); Richard Dyer, "Judy Garland and Gay Men," in *Heavenly Bodies: Film Stars and Society* (New York: St. Martin's, 1986), 141–94; Ellis Hanson, "Wilde's Exquisite Pain," in *Wilde Writings: Contextual Conditions,* ed. Joseph Bristow (Toronto: University of Toronto Press, 2002), 101–23, and "Confession as Seduction: The Queer Performativity of the Cure in Sacher-Masoch's *Venus im Pelz,*" in *Performance and Performativity in German Cultural Studies,* ed. Andrew Webber (London: Peter Lang, 2003), 41–66; Earl Jackson, Jr., *Strategies of Deviance: Studies in Gay Male Representation* (Bloomington: Indiana University Press, 1995); Wayne Koestenbaum, *The Queen's Throat: Opera, Homosexuality, and the Mystery of Desire* (New York: Poseidon Press, 1993); Kevin Kopelson, *Beethoven's Kiss: Pianism, Perversion, and the Mastery of Desire* (Stanford: Stanford University Press, 1996); Heather Love, *Feeling Backward: Loss and the Politics of Queer History* (Cambridge, MA: Harvard University Press, 2007); Biddy Martin, *Femininity Played Straight: The Significance of Being Lesbian* (New York: Routledge, 1996); Michael Warner, *The Trouble with Normal: Sex, Politics, and the Ethics of Queer Life* (New York: Free Press, 1999). A collective effort to address matters of lesbian and gay affect can be found in *Gay Shame,* ed. David M. Halperin and Valerie Traub (Chicago: University of Chicago Press, 2009). An example of both the promises and the perils of inquiring into gay subjectivity is provided by Brett Farmer, *Spectacular Passions: Cinema, Fantasy, Gay Male Spectatorships* (Durham, NC: Duke University Press, 2000).

2. J. Michael Bailey, "Homosexuality and Mental Illness," *Archives of General Psychiatry* 56.10 (1999): 883–84 (quotation on p. 884). I owe this citation to Michele Elaine Morales, "Persistent Pathologies: The Odd Coupling of Alcoholism and Homosexuality in the Discourses of Twentieth Century Science," Ph.D. diss., University of Michigan, 2006, 186.

3. See the powerful and moving firsthand testimony by Martin Duberman, *Cures: A Gay Man's Odyssey* (New York: Dutton/Plume, 1991). See, further, Henry Abelove, "Freud, Male Homosexuality, and the Americans," in *The Lesbian and Gay Studies Reader,* ed. Henry Abelove, Michèle Aina Barale, and David M. Halperin (New York: Routledge, 1993), 381–93.

4. Starting in the 1990s, however, the pendulum swung back in the other direction, and the major figures in queer theory now base much of their critical work in psychoanalysis. I am thinking in particular of Leo Bersani, Judith Butler, Lee Edelman, Diana Fuss, Teresa de Lauretis, Earl Jackson, Tim Dean, and Christopher Lane. Within queer theory, they are in the vast majority. Those who favor other approaches are rare: chiefly, D. A. Miller, Michael Warner, Paul Morrison, Ellis Hanson, and myself. Eve Sedgwick, despite her resistance to psychoanalysis, has in the last decade championed psychology: see Eve Kosofsky Sedgwick and Adam Frank, "Shame in the Cybernetic Fold: Reading Silvan Tomkins," in *Shame and Its Sisters: A Silvan Tomkins Reader,* ed. Sedgwick and Frank (Durham, NC: Duke University Press, 1995), 1–28, and Eve Kosofsky Sedgwick, *A Dialogue on Love* (Boston: Beacon Press, 1999). The queer vogue for psychoanalysis does not mean that the concrete opera-

tions of queer subjectivity are now front and center in queer studies, except in the work of Bersani, Dean, and Sedgwick.

5. Foucault made this remark in the course of a 1981 interview with the filmmaker Werner Schroeter, published by the Goethe Institute in Paris in 1982. See Michel Foucault, "Conversation avec Werner Schroeter," in *Dits et écrits 1954–1988*, ed. Daniel Defert and François Ewald (Paris: Gallimard, 1994), 4:251–60 (quotation on p. 256).

6. It is no accident that all these writers are known for the cultivation and elaboration of a literary and aesthetic style: on Style as a refuge from the Person, and thus from a stigmatized identity and a tainted psychology, see D. A. Miller, *Jane Austen, or The Secret of Style* (Princeton: Princeton University Press, 2003). For aestheticism as an alternative to psychology and psychoanalysis, see Hanson, "Wilde's Exquisite Pain" and "Confession as Seduction." On the latter phases of this anti-psychological tradition, with particular attention to Roland Barthes, see Didier Eribon, *Échapper à la psychanalyse* (Paris: Éditions Léo Scheer, 2005). Any serious effort to sustain the broad claim about the six gay writers mentioned in the text and their attempts to represent subjectivity without recourse to psychology would of course require a separate and lengthy argument.

For an excellent survey of other traditions of political reflection about subjectivity, see Barry D. Adam, "Domination, Resistance, and Subjectivity," in *The Blackwell Companion to Social Inequalities*, ed. Mary Romero and Eric Margolis (Malden, MA: Blackwell, 2005), 100–114.

7. A transcript of these lectures has now been published: Michel Foucault, *L'Herméneutique du sujet. Cours au Collège de France, 1981–1982*, ed. Frédéric Gros (Paris: Seuil/Gallimard, 2001); *The Hermeneutics of the Subject: Lectures at the Collège de France, 1981–1982*, trans. Graham Burchell (New York: Picador, 2005).

8. Foucault, *L'Herméneutique du sujet*, 444; *Hermeneutics of the Subject*, 462.

9. Foucault's course summary is included with the published transcript of his lectures: see *L'Herméneutique du sujet*, 481; *Hermeneutics of the Subject*, 501.

10. See Foucault, *L'Herméneutique du sujet*, 267–68, 277, 286–88; *Hermeneutics of the Subject*, 278–79, 289, 299–301.

11. Foucault, *L'Herméneutique du sujet*, 242–43; *Hermeneutics of the Subject*, 253.

12. Foucault, *L'Herméneutique du sujet*, 317; *Hermeneutics of the Subject*, 333. See, further, *L'Herméneutique du sujet*, 344–48;

Hermeneutics of the Subject, 362–66. Foucault explicitly exempts Freud and Lacan from his generalizations about psychology and psychoanalysis, asserting specifically that Lacan reintroduced the problem of the subject's relation to truth: see *L'Herméneutique du sujet*, 31, 182; *Hermeneutics of the Subject*, 30, 189.

13. Foucault, *L'Herméneutique du sujet*, 241; *Hermeneutics of the Subject*, 251.

14. See, for example, Michel Foucault, "An Aesthetics of Existence," in *Politics, Philosophy, Culture: Interviews and Other Writings, 1977–1984,* ed. Lawrence D. Kritzman (New York: Routledge, 1988), 47–53. For additional commentary, see Arnold I. Davidson, "Ethics as Ascetics: Foucault, the History of Ethics, and Ancient Thought," in *Foucault and the Writing of History,* ed. Jan Goldstein (Oxford: Basil Blackwell, 1994), 63–80, 266–71; and David M. Halperin, *Saint Foucault: Towards a Gay Hagiography* (New York: Oxford University Press, 1995), 67–81.

15. For the latter, see Leo Bersani, "Sociability and Cruising," *UMBR(a): A Journal of the Unconscious* (2002: "Sameness"), 9–23, esp. 21–22.

16. I refer here to my more extended argument to this effect in "Forgetting Foucault," in *How to Do the History of Homosexuality* (Chicago: University of Chicago Press, 2002), 24–47, 159–70; also, "The Normalization of Queer Theory," *Journal of Homosexuality* 45.2–4 (2003) = *Queer Theory and Communication: From Disciplining Queers to Queering the Discipline(s),* ed. Gust A. Yep, Karen E. Lovaas, and John P. Elia (New York: Haworth Press, 2003), 339–43.

17. For a now-venerable example, see the manifesto by Julian Henriques, Wendy Hollway, Cathy Urwin, Venn Couze, and Valerie Walkerdine, *Changing the Subject: Psychology, Social Regulation and Subjectivity* (London: Methuen, 1984).

18. Graham Richards, *Putting Psychology in its Place: A Critical Historical Overview,* 2d ed. (London: Routledge, 2002), 4, distinguishes between Psychology as a discipline and what he terms "its subject matter," which he designates by means of "psychology" with a lowercase *p*. My use of capital and lowercase letters is designed to distinguish instead between the formal and informal practices (or between the formal and informal discourses) of psychology.

19. For a critique of psychoanalysis on this score from within psychoanalysis, see Jean Allouch, *Érotique du deuil au temps de la mort sèche,* 2d ed. (Paris: EPEL, 1997). For an example of a non-psychological, queer language of love, see David M. Halperin, "Love's Irony: Six Remarks on Platonic Eros," in *Erotikon: Essays on Eros,*

Ancient and Modern, ed. Shadi Bartsch and Thomas Bartscherer (Chicago: University of Chicago Press, 2005), 48–58.

20. For a dose of healthy skepticism, from within the field of psychology, about the benefits of self-esteem, and a challenge to the entire self-esteem industry, see Roy F. Baumeister, Jennifer D. Campbell, Joachim I. Krueger, and Kathleen D. Vohs, "Does High Self-Esteem Cause Better Performance, Interpersonal Success, Happiness, or Healthier Lifestyles?" *Psychological Science in the Public Interest* 4.1 (May 2003): 1–44.

21. Centers for Disease Control and Prevention, *HIV/AIDS Surveillance Report,* vol. 17: *Cases of HIV Infection and AIDS in the United States and Dependent Areas, 2005* (Atlanta: U.S. Department of Health and Human Services, 2006), 34–35 (table 16), and 47; Centers for Disease Control and Prevention, *HIV/AIDS Surveillance Report,* vol. 18: *Cases of HIV Infection and AIDS in the United States and Dependent Areas, 2006* (Atlanta: U.S. Department of Health and Human Services, 2008), 5. The CDC also excludes the results of anonymous HIV testing from its statistics.

22. Nimmons, *Soul Beneath the Skin* (note 1, above), 59–61 (quotation on p. 59). Tim Dean, *Beyond Sexuality* (Chicago: University of Chicago Press, 2000), 136, echoes this statistic, summarizing other studies, as do Paul Flowers, "Gay Men and HIV/AIDS Risk Management," *Health* 5.1 (2001): 50–75, esp. 60; and Jeffrey T. Parsons, Perry N. Halkitis, Richard J. Wolitski, Cynthia A. Gómez, and the Seropositive Urban Men's Study Team, "Correlates of Sexual Risk Behaviors among HIV-Positive Men Who Have Sex with Men," *AIDS Education and Prevention* 15.5 (October 2003): 383–400, esp. 383–84, for HIV-positive gay and bisexual men.

23. For this distinction, see Susan Kippax, June Crawford, Mark Davis, Pam Rodden, and Gary Dowsett, "Sustaining Safe Sex: A Longitudinal Study of a Sample of Homosexual Men," *AIDS* 7.2 (1993): 257–63, esp. 261.

24. On the various factors that determine exactly how likely any particular act of sex is to transmit HIV, see the studies cited by Gregory Tomso, "Bug Chasing, Barebacking, and the Risks of Care," *Literature and Medicine* 23.1 (Spring 2004): 88–111, esp. 109 n. 14. These are the very sorts of factors that often enter into gay men's calculations of risk.

25. See Paul Van de Ven, Patrick Rawstorne, June Crawford, and Susan Kippax, "Increasing Proportions of Australian Gay and Homosexually Active Men Engage in Unprotected Anal Intercourse with Regular and with Casual Partners," *AIDS Care* 14.3 (2002):

335–41, cautioning that "we avoid describing these upturns in UAI-R [unprotected anal intercourse with regular partners] as increases in sexual risk practice *per se*" (339) and emphasizing that "the majority of Australian gay and homosexually active men have *no* unprotected anal intercourse during a defined interval" (340). Similarly, Barry D. Adam, Winston Husbands, James Murray, and John Maxwell, "AIDS Optimism, Condom Fatigue, or Self-Esteem? Explaining Unsafe Sex among Gay and Bisexual Men," *Journal of Sex Research* 42.3 (August 2005): 238–48, note that "74.7% of MSM [men who have sex with men] in the Toronto area report using only safe sex practices with casual partners in the past 3 months, and 54.9% report having only safe sex with regular partners" (240), citing the Ontario Men's Survey.

Somewhat higher figures for risky sex are reported by Beryl A. Koblin, Margaret A. Chesney, Marla J. Husnik, Sam Bozeman et al., "High-Risk Behaviors among Men Who Have Sex with Men in 6 US Cities: Baseline Data from the EXPLORE Study," *American Journal of Public Health* 93.6 (June 2003): 926–32, but the data are hard to assess because, as the authors acknowledge, they deliberately recruited "a large cohort of high-risk MSM" (930) for reasons unrelated to our concerns here and because they did not assess the extent to which sexual behavior took place in a context of "negotiated safety" (931). (For the original and authoritative definition of "negotiated safety," see note 51, below.)

For more detailed information about the percentage of HIV-negative gay men who take significant risks in their sexual practices, see note 40, below.

26. As Michael Shernoff observes, summarizing the epidemiological literature, most unprotected sex among gay men takes place with regular sexual partners in the context of committed relationships: see Shernoff, *Without Condoms: Unprotected Sex, Gay Men & Barebacking* (New York: Routledge, 2006), 181–85. But as Shernoff also notes, following Troy Suarez and Jeffrey Miller, "Negotiating Risks in Context: A Perspective on Unprotected Anal Intercourse and Barebacking Among Men Who Have Sex with Men—Where Do We Go from Here?" *Archives of Sexual Behavior* 30.3 (2001): 287–300, esp. 288, the term *barebacking* tends to be applied to gay men's unprotected anal intercourse with casual or anonymous partners. (Shernoff's study focuses on the United States, but his analysis may be valid for gay men elsewhere, as Barry D. Adam notes in his review of the book in *Sexuality Research & Social Policy* 3.4 [December 2006]: 94–95.)

27. For the recent rise in annual diagnoses of HIV/AIDS, see

the CDC's latest analyses in its *HIV/AIDS Surveillance Reports* for 2005 and 2006 (note 21, above), table 1 (pp. 10 and 11, respectively). These figures, which refer to the year of reported diagnosis, not the year of actual infection, are based on information from the thirty-three states and five U.S. territories with a long-term track record of confidential name-based reporting of HIV infection; they have been adjusted for reporting errors and constitute the most reliable aggregate figures for the number of people diagnosed each year with HIV and/or AIDS that the CDC possesses—even though they represent, by the CDC's own estimate, only 63 percent of the epidemic in the United States (see p. 5 of each of the last two annual reports).

By contrast, the figures for newly diagnosed cases of AIDS in the *entire* United States and its territories represent estimates. Nationally, according to the CDC's latest adjusted calculation, cases of AIDS that can be ascribed to male-to-male sexual transmission decreased 2.3 percent from 2003 to 2005 and then rose nearly 2 percent in 2006 (see p. 13, table 3)—or, as the CDC puts it in its annual surveillance report for 2006, "The numbers of males exposed through male-to-male sexual contact . . . remained stable" (7).

It should be noted that the CDC has a history of issuing alarmist reports about increases in new cases of HIV/AIDS in gay and bisexual men, reports which often make the news but are later—quietly—corrected. For example, in 2005, the CDC had called attention, quite reasonably at the time, to a frightening 8 percent increase during the previous year in newly diagnosed cases of HIV infection and/or AIDS due to male-to-male sexual transmission. See "Trends in HIV/AIDS Diagnoses—33 States, 2001–2004," *Morbidity and Mortality Weekly Report* (Centers for Disease Control and Prevention), 54.45 (November 18, 2005): 1149–53, esp. 1150: "From 2003 to 2004, the number of HIV/AIDS diagnoses among MSM increased 8%; this increase was statistically significant (p<0.05)." Even at the time, however, the CDC had cautioned, in an editorial comment on the report, "Whereas increases among MSM might reflect increases in HIV incidence, consistent with increases in syphilis and other risk behaviors, they might also reflect increases in HIV testing among MSM" (p. 1153). The CDC has now revised that figure downward from 8 percent to just over 3 percent. Similarly, in its annual surveillance report for 2005, the CDC had recorded a horrific 13 percent rise during the period 2004–2005 in HIV/AIDS diagnoses among MSM in thirty-three American states as well as in the total number of estimated new cases of AIDS diagnosed in the entire United States, but now, in its annual surveillance report for 2006, it calculates that the increase in 2005 in diagnoses of

HIV/AIDS due to male-to-male sexual transmission in the thirty-three states was in fact 6 percent (which is bad enough), whereas there was an actual *decrease* of more than 2 percent in the total number of estimated new diagnoses of AIDS among MSM in the United States as a whole.

This progressive downward revision of the CDC's published numbers results from nothing more sinister than the removal of duplicate cases from its database and the replacement of earlier estimates, made to compensate for delays in reporting, with new hard data. Because of the statistical procedures the CDC uses to calculate its annual estimates, and because of the lapse of time required for the CDC to adjust them in the light of newer data, the figures for cases of HIV/AIDS diagnosed in the most recent year of the reporting cycle tend to be overestimates and are likely to be revised progressively downward by the CDC in the coming years. So they should be used with caution.

Nonetheless, the documented rise in the numbers of newly diagnosed cases of HIV infection and/or AIDS among men who have sex with men in a majority of American states from 2003 through 2006 is disturbing and it should arouse real concern. The latest, revised estimates for the period from 2001 to 2006 provided by A. Mitsch et al., "Trends in HIV/AIDS Diagnoses Among Men Who Have Sex with Men—33 States, 2001–2006," *Morbidity and Mortality Weekly Report,* 57.25 (June 27, 2008): 681–86, indicate that "the number of HIV/AIDS diagnoses among MSM overall during 2001–2006 increased 8.6%" (681), with men who have sex with men constituting the single largest transmission category as well as the only one associated with an increasing number of HIV/AIDS diagnoses (683).

28. See Jonathan Elford, "Changing Patterns of Sexual Behaviour in the Era of Highly Active Antiretroviral Therapy," *Current Opinion in Infectious Diseases* 19 (2006): 26–32, esp. 28–29. On the last point mentioned, see, for example, P. Keogh, S. Beardsell, and Sigma Research, "Sexual Negotiation Strategies of HIV-Positive Gay Men: A Qualitative Approach," in *AIDS: Activism and Alliances,* ed. Peter Aggleton, Graham Hart, and Peter Davies (London: Taylor & Francis, 1997), 226–37, cited, discussed, and corroborated by Ian Hodges and Eamonn Rodohan, "Living with Homophobia: Exploring Accounts of Communication and Disclosure from London Gay Men Diagnosed with HIV," *Lesbian and Gay Psychology Review* 5.3 (November 2004): 109–17; similarly, "High-Risk Sexual Behavior by HIV-Positive Men Who Have Sex with Men—16 Sites, United States, 2000–2002," *Morbidity and Mortal-*

ity Weekly Report (Centers for Disease Control and Prevention), 53.38 (October 1, 2004): 891–94: "findings indicated that a large percentage of HIV-positive MSM were sexually abstinent, practiced safer sexual behavior by having protected insertive anal intercourse, or had UIAI with an HIV-positive partner. . . . Nonetheless, UIAI occurred in 6% of the sexual encounters with HIV-negative and unknown serostatus partners" (891, 894). Parsons et al., "Correlates of Risk Behaviors" (note 22, above), 390–92, also found that only 6.3 percent of HIV-positive men in New York and San Francisco reported practicing insertive anal intercourse with a non-primary partner known to be HIV-negative; similarly, Elford reports that "a 2002–2003 study in London among HIV-positive men attending a public HIV treatment clinic found that in the previous 12 months 5% of HIV-positive men had intentionally looked for UAI with a person of unknown or discordant HIV status" (28). For more details, see Perry N. Halkitis, Kelly A. Green, Robert H. Remien, Michael J. Stirratt, Colleen C. Hoff, Richard J. Wolitski, and Jeffrey T. Parsons, "Seroconcordant Sexual Partnerings of HIV-Seropositive Men Who Have Sex with Men," *AIDS* 19, Supplement 1 (2005): S77–S86; and Jeffrey T. Parsons, Eric W. Schrimshaw, Richard J. Wolitski, Perry N. Halkitis, David W. Purcell, Colleen C. Hoff, and Cynthia A. Gómez, "Sexual Harm Reduction Practices of HIV-Seropositive Gay and Bisexual Men: Serosorting, Strategic Positioning, and Withdrawal before Ejaculation," *AIDS* 19, Supplement 1 (2005): S13–S25.

One study of a population of HIV-positive gay and bisexual men in New York and San Francisco who all identified themselves explicitly as "barebackers," and who had all had sex with at least one partner of HIV-negative or unknown serostatus during the previous year, found that 57 percent of that population reported having had bareback sex with partners of negative or unknown serostatus, but such a finding is not typical of HIV-positive gay men overall: see Perry N. Halkitis, Leo Wilton, Richard J. Wolitski, Jeffrey T. Parsons, Colleen C. Hoff, and David S. Bimbi, "Barebacking Identity among HIV-Positive Gay and Bisexual Men: Demographic, Psychological, and Behavioral Correlates," *AIDS,* 19, Supplement 1 (2005): S27–S35.

More worrisome is a study of HIV-positive men who have sex with men, conducted from 1995 to 2000 in twelve U.S. states, which found that among men who were well aware of their positive serostatus, and who also had "a single steady male partner with negative or unknown serostatus," more than one-fifth (21 percent) had engaged in unprotected anal intercourse with that partner in the previous twelve months; the study recruited a large proportion of minority or underprivileged men, and it found that "no education beyond high school, heterosexual self-identification, and crack cocaine use" were factors predictive of UAI: see Paul H. Denning and Michael L. Campsmith, "Unprotected Anal Intercourse Among HIV-Positive Men Who Have a Steady Male Sex Partner With Negative or Unknown HIV Serostatus," *American Journal of Public Health* 95.1 (January 2005): 152–58, esp. 154.

29. Davey M. Smith, Douglas D. Richman, and Susan J. Little, "HIV Superinfection," *Journal of Infectious Diseases* 192.3 (August 2005): 438–44 (quotation on p. 442). See, further, Matthew J. Gonzales, Eric Delwart, Soo-Yon Rhee, Rose Tsui, Andrew R. Zolopa, Jonathan Taylor, and Robert W. Shafer, "Lack of Detectable Human Immunodeficiency Virus Type 1 Superinfection during 1072 Person-Years of Observation," *Journal of Infectious Diseases* 188.3 (August 1, 2003): 397–405; Rose Tsui, Belinda L. Herring, Jason D. Barbour, Robert M. Grant, Peter Bacchetti, Alex Kral, Brian R. Edlin, and Eric L. Delwart, "Human Immunodeficiency Virus Type 1 Superinfection Was Not Detected following 215 Years of Injection Drug User Exposure," *Journal of Virology* 78.1 (January 2004): 94–103; Shernoff, *Without Condoms,* 222–23.

30. See Christopher Heredia, "A Serosorting Story: Dating within the HIV Positive or Negative Population Has Reduced the HIV Infection Rate in San Francisco. It Also Allows for an Intimacy Previously Missing," *San Francisco Chronicle,* February 12, 2006. Heredia may be overplaying the data, however: the CDC report on which his story seems to be based ("HIV Prevalence, Unrecognized Infection, and HIV Testing Among Men Who Have Sex with Men—Five U.S. Cities, June 2004–April 2005," *Morbidity and Mortality Weekly Report* [Centers for Disease Control and Prevention], 54.24 [June 24, 2005]: 597–601) does not in fact provide sound statistics for HIV transmission rates in San Francisco as a whole, and the crediting of serosorting with the claimed decline in HIV transmission is the conclusion drawn not by the CDC but by Dr. Mitch Katz, San Francisco's public health director. Some support for the efficacy of serosorting is provided by H. M. Truong, T. Kellogg, J. D. Klausner, M. H. Katz, J. Dilley, K. Knapper, S. Chen, R. Prabhu, R. M. Grant, B. Louie, and W. McFarland, "Increases in Sexually Transmitted Infections and Sexual Risk Behaviour without a Concurrent Increase in HIV Incidence among Men Who Have Sex with Men in San Francisco: A Suggestion of HIV Serosorting?" *Sexually Transmitted Infections,* 82.6 (December 1, 2006), 461–66, who cautiously conclude that "HIV incidence

among MSM appears to have stabilised at a plateau following several years of resurgence. Increases in the selection of sexual partners of concordant HIV serostatus may be contributing to the stabilisation of the epidemic. However, current incidence rates of STI and HIV remain high." During a slightly earlier period, some members of Truong's team had similarly reported an increase in cases of syphilis among men who have sex with men in San Francisco and Los Angeles without a concurrent increase in HIV incidence: see "Trends in Primary and Secondary Syphilis and HIV Infections in Men Who Have Sex with Men—San Francisco and Los Angeles, California, 1998–2002," *Morbidity and Mortality Weekly Report,* 53.26 (July 9, 2004), 575–78.

Another local study that offers a basis in epidemiological evidence for regarding serosorting as a possible safer sex technique has been produced by Matthew R. Golden, Devon D. Brewer, Ann Kurth, King K. Holmes, and H. Hunter Handsfield, "Importance of Sex Partner HIV Status in HIV Risk Assessment Among Men Who have Sex With Men," *Journal of Acquired Immune Deficiency Syndromes* 36.2 (June 1, 2004): 734–42, esp. 740: "Restricting UAI to partners believed to be HIV-negative is protective, although a substantial risk of HIV persists." Beena Varghese, Julie E. Maher, Thomas A. Peterman, Bernard M. Branson, and Richard W. Steketee, "Reducing the Risk of Sexual HIV Transmission," *Sexually Transmitted Diseases* 29.1 (2002): 38–43, argue that partner choice is the most effective safe sex technique, but their conclusion is based on a purely theoretical model and is of little value.

On serosorting more generally, see Elford, "Changing Patterns" (note 28, above), 28–29, and the literature cited by Duncan A. MacKellar et al., "Unintentional HIV Exposures from Young Men Who Have Sex with Men Who Disclose Being HIV-Negative," *AIDS* 20.12 (August 1, 2006): 1637–44.

31. See Zak Szymanski, "HIV Campaigns Spark Debate," *Bay Area Reporter,* November 9, 2006, and www.disclosehiv.org.

32. Kane Race, "Engaging in a Culture of Barebacking: Gay Men and the Risk of HIV Prevention," in *Gendered Risks,* ed. Kelly Hannah-Moffat and Pat O'Malley (London: Routledge-Cavendish, 2007), 99–126.

33. In order for barebacking among seroconcordant partners to function as an effective risk reduction practice, it is of course crucial that those who believe themselves to be HIV-negative actually know their correct serostatus, that they really be HIV-negative, but this is all too often not the case in metropolitan centers of the United States. On the numbers of young HIV-positive men who

have sex with men, but who do not know their serostatus or mistakenly believe themselves to be HIV-negative, see Richard J. Wolitski, "The Emergence of Barebacking Among Gay and Bisexual Men in the United States: A Public Health Perspective," *Journal of Gay & Lesbian Psychotherapy* 9.3–4 (2005): 9–34, esp. 26; for indications that many young infected men in U.S. cities are unaware of being infected with HIV, see "HIV Prevalence, Unrecognized Infection" (note 30 above). According to MacKellar et al., "Unintentional HIV Exposures" (note 30, above), 1638, summarizing an earlier study of his conducted between 1994 and 2000, "Among 15–29-year-old MSM recruited in six US cities, for example, [of whom 10 percent tested positive for HIV], 77% of 573 HIV-infected MSM were unaware of their infection," although 82 percent of them had previously been tested: see Duncan A. MacKellar, Linda A. Valleroy, Gina M. Secura, Stephanie Behel, Trista Bingham, David D. Celentano et al., "Unrecognized HIV Infection, Risk Behaviors, and Perceptions of Risk Among Young Men Who Have Sex With Men: Opportunities for Advancing HIV Prevention in the Third Decade of HIV/AIDS," *Journal of Acquired Immune Deficiency Syndromes* 38.5 (April 15, 2005): 603–14; the authors acknowledge, however, that "our reported magnitude of unrecognized infection among young MSM is upwardly biased to some unknown extent" (612). Susan Buchbinder et al., "Sexual Risk, Nitrite Inhalant Use, and Lack of Circumcision Associated With HIV Seroconversion in Men Who Have Sex With Men in the United States," *Journal of Acquired Immune Deficiency Syndromes* 39.1 (May 1, 2005): 82–89, found that "more than one quarter of new infections arose from men having HIV-'negative' partners" (86); similarly, Beryl A. Koblin et al., "Risk Factors for HIV Infection among Men Who Have Sex with Men," *AIDS* 20 (March 21, 2006): 731–39, found that "just over one-fifth of seroincidence (21.6%) was accounted for by unprotected receptive anal intercourse with partners believed to be HIV negative" (735). Those last two findings should be used with caution, however, because the studies that produced them, though up to date and mathematically sophisticated, do not distinguish between statistical "risk factors" and actual transmission pathways. For a more recent and sober study, conducted between 1998 and 2000, which found that 7 percent of young gay men who told their partners that they were uninfected with HIV actually turned out to be wrong about their serostatus ("HIV-infected unaware"), and that half of this 7 percent then went on to have unprotected anal sex, see MacKellar et al., "Unintentional HIV Exposures," 1640, who add that "HIV-infected unaware disclosers were more likely to be black, to have obtained no higher than a high-school education, and to have engaged in receptive anal sex with other men in the last 6 months." A number of studies have found that young black men are more likely than young white men to be unaware of being infected with HIV and to underestimate their chances of being infected (see MacKellar et al., "Unrecognized HIV Infection," 610).

34. I take this point from Race, "Culture of Barebacking" (note 32, above). See also Hodges and Rodohan, "Living with Homophobia" (note 28, above).

35. For detailed discussion of some examples, see Nicolas Sheon and G. Michael Crosby, "Ambivalent Tales of HIV Disclosure in San Francisco," *Social Science & Medicine* 58 (2004): 2105–18; also, P. Keogh and P. Weatherburn, "Tales from the Backroom: Anonymous Sex and HIV Risk in London's Commercial Gay Sex Venues," *Venereology* 13.4 (2000): 150–55.

36. Kane Race, personal communication, November 13, 2006.

37. Juliet Richters, ed., *HIV/AIDS, Hepatitis and Sexually Transmissible Infections in Australia: Annual Report of Trends in Behaviour 2006* (Sydney: National Centre in HIV Social Research, 2006), 52. See, further, Limin Mao, June M. Crawford, Harm J. Hospers, Garrett P. Prestage, Andrew E. Grulich, John M. Kaldor, and Susan C. Kippax, "'Serosorting' in Casual Anal Sex of HIV-Negative Gay Men is Noteworthy and is Increasing in Sydney, Australia," *AIDS*, 20.8 (May 12, 2006), 1204–1206, who observed an increase over time in the proportion of unprotected anal intercourse with casual partners among HIV-negative gay men attributable to serosorting and who call attention to the risks associated with this practice.

38. See, for example, Christian Grov, "'Make Me Your Death Slave': Men Who Have Sex with Men and Use the Internet to Intentionally Spread HIV," *Deviant Behavior* 25.4 (July–August 2004): 329–49. Grov does not consider the possibility, later documented by Shernoff, *Without Condoms,* 162–63, that some men who advertise as HIV-negative bug chasers are actually HIV-positive men who seek to heighten or intensify the thrills of sex with other HIV-positive men by pretending to be HIV-negative.

39. Kane D. Race, "Revaluation of Risk among Gay Men," *AIDS Education and Prevention* 15.4 (2003): 369–81 (quotation on p. 374), citing Gordon Mansergh et al., "'Barebacking' in a Diverse Sample of Men who Have Sex with Men," *AIDS* 16.4 (March 8, 2002): 653–59; I have checked Race's tabulation for accuracy.

Wolitski, "Emergence of Barebacking" (note 33, above), lobbies for a more expansive definition of barebacking, which would take in

all intentional unprotected anal sex except that between HIV-negative men in a context of "negotiated safety." His inclusive definition
would extend the term *barebacking* to many sexual behaviors that
are intended to reduce the risk of HIV infection and would thereby
blur the distinction between behaviors that are understood to be
risky and behaviors that are intended to avoid or diminish risk by
those who practice them.

Studies of HIV-positive gay and bisexual men yield a higher percentage of those who fail to use condoms consistently in insertive
anal sex with partners who are HIV-negative or of unknown HIV
status, but still no more than about a quarter of the sample: see
Barry D. Adam, "Constructing the Neoliberal Sexual Actor:
Responsibility and Care of the Self in the Discourse of Barebackers," *Culture, Health & Sexuality* 7.4 (July–August 2005): 333–46,
esp. 338, citing Parsons et al., "Correlates of Risk Behaviors" (note
22, above), 392, 394, to which add p. 384; even so, only 6.3 percent
of HIV-positive men in New York and San Francisco reported practicing insertive anal intercourse with a nonprimary partner known
to be HIV-negative (Parsons et al., 390–92). For other studies that
confirm this picture, see note 28, above. In any case, these HIV-positive men incur little risk themselves, and so they do not raise the
same questions about "self-destructiveness" that cluster about the
risk-taking activities of HIV-negative men who bareback, which is
why they do not figure in the discussion here.

40. Only 12.1 percent of HIV-negative men in a San Francisco
study conducted between 1999 and 2001 reported practicing unprotected anal intercourse with "potentially serodiscordant" partners,
according to Sanny Y. Chen, Steven Gibson, Darlene Weide, and
Willi McFarland, "Unprotected Anal Intercourse between Potentially HIV-Serodiscordant Men Who Have Sex With Men, San
Francisco," *Journal of Acquired Immune Deficiency Syndromes* 33.2
(June 1, 2003): 166–70, even though other reports indicate that UAI
is coming to be a community norm among some gay men in San
Francisco (on this point, see Sheon and Crosby, "Ambivalent Tales"
[note 35, above]). A recent telephone survey conducted in Seattle
likewise produced a figure of 10 percent of HIV-negative MSM who
had had UAI in the previous twelve months with at least one man
believed to be HIV-positive or of unknown serostatus: see Devon
D. Brewer, Matthew R. Golden, and H. Hunter Handsfield,
"Unsafe Sexual Behavior and Correlates of Risk in a Probability
Sample of Men Who Have Sex With Men in the Era of Highly
Active Antiretroviral Therapy," *Sexually Transmitted Diseases* 33.4
(2006): 250–55. A 1999 survey of seven thousand homosexually

active men in New York City also found that only 11 percent "reported having unprotected sex with men with a different or unknown HIV status," according to Nimmons, *Soul Beneath the Skin,* 65, citing T. W. Mayne et al., *Beyond 2000 Sexual Health Survey: Sexual Health and Practices of Gay, Bisexual and Homosexually Active Men in New York City* (New York: Gay Men's Health Crisis, 1999). A similar figure for the percentage of HIV-negative gay men in the United States as a whole who have unprotected sex with possibly infected men has been recently provided by Travis Sanchez et al., "Human Immunodeficiency Virus (HIV) Risk, Prevention, and Testing Behaviors—United States, National HIV Behavioral Surveillance System: Men Who Have Sex with Men, November 2003–April 2005," *Morbidity and Mortality Weekly Report* (Centers for Disease Control and Prevention), 55.SS-6 (July 7, 2006): 1–16, who found that "approximately 11% of HIV-negative participants reported having unprotected anal sex with a partner whose HIV status was unknown" (11).

More alarming are recent figures from Australia for aggregate practices of unprotected anal intercourse with casual partners by HIV-negative men. About a quarter of such men report UAI with casual partners, and that percentage remained fairly constant throughout the years 2000–2004 inclusive: see Patrick Rawstorne, Carla Treloar, and Juliet Richters, ed., *Annual Report of Behaviour 2005: HIV/AIDS, Hepatitis and Sexually Transmissible Infections in Australia,* National Centre in HIV Social Research, Monograph 3/2005 (Sydney: National Centre in HIV Social Research, 2005), p. 18, table 1.1.10. The aggregate nature of that data, however, does not allow exact assessments of risk: no distinctions can be drawn among HIV-negative men who barebacked deliberately; men who had unprotected sex regularly; men who had unprotected sex once in the previous six months, possibly unintentionally; and men whose partners were HIV-negative; it is also impossible to distinguish between men who had insertive unprotected anal sex and men who had receptive unprotected anal sex. Therefore it would be incautious to draw alarmist conclusions from this data without further analysis. However, Limin Mao et al., "'Serosorting'" (note 37, above), show that some of this increase in UAIC on the part of HIV-negative gay men is attributable to serosorting (which, of course, does not indicate that it is risk-free).

Similarly, 26 percent of HIV-negative men who frequented sex-on-premises venues in and around Paris in 2005 self-reported at least one episode of unprotected anal sex with casual partners in the previous twelve months; the population is not representative, however, and once again the aggregate nature of the data does not allow accurate measurement of actual risk: see Annie Velter, Alice Bouyssou-Michel, Josiane Pillonel, Guy Jacquier, and Caroline Semaille, "Baromètre gay 2005: enquête auprès des hommes fréquentant les lieux de rencontre gay franciliens," *Bulletin épidémiologique hebdomadaire* 25 (2006): 178–80 (see p. 179, table 2).

41. See Alvin G. Dawson, Jr., Michael W. Ross, Doug Henry, and Anne Freeman, "Evidence of HIV Transmission Risk in Barebacking Men-Who-Have-Sex-With-Men: Cases from the Internet," *Journal of Gay & Lesbian Psychotherapy* 9.3–4 (2005): 73–83, esp. 81: "These data suggest that the large majority of cases advertising for bareback sex, even in a worst-case scenario, involve assortative serostatus interactions [i.e., serosorting] and are specifically designed to minimize HIV transmission. Only in one case was a clear preference by a HIV positive individual for an HIV negative individual expressed. We conclude, on the face of these data, that the level of deliberate HIV transmission ('gift giving' or 'bug chasing') in barebacking within this sample is extremely low, although the potential for indifferent transmission is unacceptably high." Both aspects of this conclusion (the lack of deliberate intent to infect or be infected with HIV but the high rate of indifference to the possibility of HIV infection on the part of bareback website users) have been massively confirmed by Shernoff, *Without Condoms* (note 26, above), 157–64 and 318–19, who also draws on work by Grov, "Make Me Your Death Slave" (note 38, above) and by Richard Tewksbury, "Bareback Sex and the Quest for HIV: Assessing the Relationship in Internet Personal Advertisements of Men Who Have Sex with Men," *Deviant Behavior* 24.5 (September–October 2003): 467–82, who found that "less than 1% of uninfected men say they are seeking an infected partner, and less than 2% of infected men are specifically seeking an uninfected partner" (477). Similar statistics have been reported for gay and bisexual men both on and off the internet. "In an online survey of more than 2500 MSM, only 1.9% reported that they had ever had anal sex without a condom because they wanted to get HIV," according to Patrick S. Sullivan and Richard J. Wolitski, "HIV Infection among Gay and Bisexual Men," in *Unequal Opportunity: Health Disparities Affecting Gay and Bisexual Men in the United States,* ed. Richard J. Wolitski, Ron Stall, and Ronald O. Valdiserri (Oxford: Oxford University Press, 2008), 220–47 (quotation on p. 228), citing an unpublished paper by Wolitski and his collaborators.

42. Michael Gross, "When Plagues Don't End," *American Journal of Public Health* 93.6 (June 2003): 861–62, remarks, "To prevent

HIV transmission, we have little more today than we had 2 decades ago, when it became clear that the virus causing AIDS is sexually transmitted: behavioral interventions" (quotation on p. 861). Similarly, Susan Kippax, "A Public Health Dilemma: A Testing Question," *AIDS Care,* 18.3 (April 2006), 230–35, observes, "Behavioural prevention is the most effective 'vaccine' we have. . . ." (quotation on p. 230).

43. I can testify from firsthand experience in San Francisco in 1983 to the early discovery and dissemination of safe sex protocols by gay communities in the United States. See also Flowers, "Gay Men" (note 22, above); Jeffrey Escoffier, "The Invention of Safer Sex: Vernacular Knowledge, Gay Politics and HIV Prevention," *Berkeley Journal of Sociology* 43 (1999): 1–30; Marsha Rosengarten, Kane Race, and Susan Kippax, *"Touch Wood, Everything Will Be OK": Gay Men's Understandings of Clinical Markers in Sexual Practice,* National Centre in HIV Social Research, Monograph 7/2000 (Sydney: National Centre in HIV Social Research, 2000); Susan Kippax and Kane Race, "Sustaining Safe Practice: Twenty Years On," *Social Science & Medicine* 57.1 (2003): 1–12, esp. 2; Barry D. Adam, Winston Husbands, James Murray, and John Maxwell, "Risk Construction in the Reinfection Discourses of HIV-Positive Men," *Health, Risk & Society* 7.1 (March 2005): 63–71.

44. See Thomas J. Coates et al., "HIV Prevention in Developed Countries," *The Lancet,* 348.9035 (October 26, 1996): 1143–48, cited by Kippax and Race, "Sustaining Safe Practice: Twenty Years On" (see previous note), who adduce more recent evidence to the same effect.

45. Ron D. Stall, Thomas J. Coates, and Colleen Hoff, "Behavioral Risk Reduction for HIV Infection among Gay and Bisexual Men: A Review of Results from the United States," *American Psychologist* 43.11 (November 1988): 878–85, cited and quoted by Nimmons, *Soul Beneath the Skin,* 61. Eric Rofes, however, who also quotes this passage, has argued with some plausibility that the change in gay men's sexual behavior during the 1980s may have been exaggerated: see Eric Rofes, *Reviving the Tribe: Regenerating Gay Men's Sexuality and Culture in the Ongoing Epidemic* (New York: Harrington Park Press, 1996), 145–51, 173–79, and *Dry Bones Breathe: Gay Men Creating Post-AIDS Identities and Cultures* (New York: Harrington Park Press, 1998), 199–200. Race, "Culture of Barebacking" (note 32, above), casts further doubt on the accuracy of HIV-negative gay men's self-reported practice of safe sex.

46. Rawstorne, Treloar, and Richters, *Annual Report* (note 40, above), 4.

47. Of the estimated 54,230 new HIV infections among whites, blacks, and Hispanics in 2006, 13,230 or just 24 percent were among white gay and bisexual men who were not also at risk of infection from injecting drugs, according to the CDC's latest published calculation: see J. Prejean, R. Song, Q. An, and H. I. Hall, "Subpopulation Estimates from the HIV Incidence Surveillance System—United States, 2006," *Morbidity and Mortality Weekly Report,* 57.36 (September 12, 2008): 985–89, especially the table on p. 987. This implies that white gay men represented an even smaller proportion of the overall number of new HIV infections in the United States as a whole—a point that was lost in the reporting of this study in the mainstream press, which sensationalized and mischaracterized it. For example, Elizabeth Fernandez, "Young Black Men at High Risk for HIV, CDC Says," *San Francisco Chronicle,* September 12, 2008, p. A-6, wrote, "Overall, white gay men account for almost half the number of new HIV cases." But that was to mistake the percentages of MSM newly infected with HIV, according to the CDC report, for percentages of the American population as a whole: whites did represent 46 percent of new HIV infections among men who have sex with men but *not* "amost half the number of new HIV cases" overall in the United States in 2006.

48. The Centers for Disease Control and Prevention report that men who have sex with men accounted for 49 percent of HIV/AIDS cases diagnosed in the United States in 2006, the most recent period for which the CDC has provided comprehensive figures: see CDC, *HIV/AIDS Surveillance Report,* vol. 18 (note 21, above), 6 (referring to p. 11, table 1, which seems however to yield a figure of 47.5 percent, whereas Mitsch et al., "Trends in HIV/AIDS Diagnoses" [note 27, above], 681, put the figure at 46 percent). This proportion has been increasing annually since 2001, when it was 40.5 percent, according to the CDC's annual surveillance report for 2005. Even so, those figures are based on the thirty-three states and five territories that have provided the CDC with confidential, name-based reporting of HIV infection since at least 2003; the figures represent, by the CDC's own estimate, 63 percent, or less than two-thirds, of the total epidemic in the United States (p. 5). When the CDC estimates the annual number of cases of AIDS in the entire United States and "dependent areas," not just in states and territories that furnish it with name-based reporting (p. 51), it finds that *male-to-male sexual contact accounted for only 35 percent of total AIDS cases diagnosed in 2006* and only 44 percent of all AIDS cases diagnosed in the United States from the start of the epidemic through 2006: see p. 37 (table 17). Similarly, the CDC attributed

more than 43 percent of new HIV infections in forty-five states and
five territories of the United States in 2006 to male-to-male sexual
contact (36 percent of the total from the start of the epidemic to
2006): see p. 38 (table 18). Nonetheless, the CDC *estimates* that
male-to-male sexual contact accounted for 42 percent of AIDS cases
diagnosed in the entire United States and its territories in 2006 (a
proportion which has steadily increased from just under 39 percent
in 2001), and 46 percent of the cumulative total of such cases from
the beginning of the epidemic through 2006: see p. 12 (table 3).

A recent report from the CDC estimated that from 2001 to 2004
"44% of new HIV infections [in the United States] were in MSM":
see "The Global HIV/AIDS Pandemic, 2006," *Morbidity and Mortality Weekly Report,* 55.31 (August 11, 2006): 841–44 (quotation on
p. 842). But the CDC's newly released estimate of HIV incidence in
the United States hypothesizes that men who have sex with men
accounted for a massive 53 percent of all new HIV infections in
2006: see H. Irene Hall, Ruiguang Song, Philip Rhodes et al., "Estimation of HIV Incidence in the United States," *JAMA,* 300.5
(August 6, 2008): 520–29, esp. 524. That figure is a statistical projection, however, and it remains somewhat speculative.

Furthermore, the CDC now conjectures that "HIV incidence
has been increasing steadily among gay and bisexual men since the
early 1990s" (*Estimates of New HIV Infections in the United States,*
CDC HIV/AIDS Facts, August 2008, p. 3), by which they seem to
mean total numbers of new infections each year. An independent
literature review finds that true HIV incidence (that is, rates of HIV
transmission) among MSM did not either rise or decline between
1995 and 2005 (Ronald Stall, "What's Driving the US Epidemic in
Men Who Have Sex with Men?" [paper delivered at the 15th Conference on Retroviruses and Opportunistic Infections, Boston, February 3–6, 2008, podcast accessed on August 26, 2008]).

49. Elford, "Changing Patterns" (note 28, above), 27; see also
Jonathan Elford, Graham Bolding, Lorraine Sherr, and Graham
Hart, "High-Risk Sexual Behaviour among London Gay Men: No
Longer Increasing," *AIDS* 19.18 (December 2, 2005): 2171–74, who
report that risky sexual behavior among some gay men in London,
though still higher than in 1998, may have leveled off between 2002
and 2005. For the detailed documentation of this trend in Australia
during the years 2001 to 2005 inclusive (the latest period surveyed),
see Richters, *HIV/AIDS* (note 37, above), 2, 9–16.

50. For the latest on this much-debated topic, see J. Campo, M.
A. Perea, J. del Romero, J. Cano, V. Hernando, and A. Bascones,
"Oral Transmission of HIV, Reality or Fiction? An Update," *Oral*

Diseases 12 (2006): 219–28, who emphasize the relatively low risk of HIV transmission in oral-genital contact and describe the factors that elevate or diminish the risk.

51. Susan Kippax, June Crawford, Mark Davis, Pam Rodden, and Gary Dowsett, "Sustaining Safe Sex: A Longitudinal Study" (note 23, above), 258: "While there is continuing debate about the safety of unprotected anal intercourse between seropositive men, the findings of this study demonstrate that many men use their concordant serostatuses as a means of preventing the transmission of HIV. A new term is needed, therefore, for unprotected anal intercourse (or any other sexual practice) that is safe in a particular context, even though the same activity is deemed 'unsafe' in the abstract. We suggest 'negotiated safety.'" For a more detailed discussion, see Shernoff, *Without Condoms,* 199–205, and for a summary of some critiques of the way the concept of negotiated safety has come to inform subsequent assumptions about gay men's sexual practices, see Damien Thomas Ridge, "'It was an Incredible Thrill': The Social Meanings and Dynamics of Younger Gay Men's Experiences of Barebacking in Melbourne," *Sexualities* 7.3 (2004): 259–79, esp. 261–62.

52. Race, "Culture of Barebacking." Cf. Parsons et al., "Sexual Harm Reduction Practices" (note 28, above), S23: "Gay and bisexual men are making decisions to use these strategies in the absence of complete data, and are empirically testing serosorting, strategic positioning, and withdrawal with their own bodies."

53. Shernoff, *Without Condoms,* 12.

54. I owe this point to Kane Race, specifically to his workshop at the 2006 University of Michigan conference "Against Health." See also the published warnings by Barry Adam and others to the same effect (note 95, below).

55. Tim Dean, Robert Caserio, Heather Love, and Jean-Michel Rabaté, "On Bareback Subcultures and the Pornography of Risk," *Slought Foundation Online Content* (October 6, 2006; accessed November 30, 2006), http://slought.org/content/11332/.

56. Dean et al., "On Bareback Subcultures."

57. That is the view that Tony Valenzuela and his group, Real Prevention, have been promoting, in opposition to responsibilizing HIV/AIDS prevention campaigns, such as "HIV stops with me" or the recent Los Angeles initiative, "HIV is a gay disease. Own it. End it," according to Szymanski, "HIV Campaigns Spark Debate" (note 31, above): "another possibility, say some longtime AIDS activists and educators [is] that gay men are in fact talking about HIV and taking care of each other, but that a post-crisis climate has meant

more people—positive and negative—are using harm reduction approaches and taking calculated risks they can live with. Critics of marketing said the evolution of the disease from a death sentence to a more manageable condition—combined with the declining HIV rates among gay men—mean that sex without condoms is often practiced with thought, discussion, and safety rather than recklessness. 'The tone of many of these campaigns presume [*sic*] the lowest common denominator of gay men. But the gay men I know are smart, savvy, sophisticated, and caring of one another. They are talking about HIV and interested in serosorting and knowing more of the science behind it,' said Los Angeles–based HIV activist and writer Tony Valenzuela. 'With or without the blessing of health departments and AIDS service organizations, men are figuring out how to have the sex they want to have more safely. Some are choosing only oral sex. Some [negatives] are choosing unprotected sex only if they top. Just because things have improved doesn't mean people think it's no big deal. I have spoken with people who understand HIV to be a manageable disease but who still do not want to get it. But it's reasonable to assume that if the meds continue to get better, and there is a reduced threat of HIV, people will be taking calculated risks as a means of harm reduction and HIV prevention.'" For a cautionary rejoinder, see Kane Race's remarks quoted in note 107, below.

Cf. Suarez and Miller (note 26, above), who offer a balanced approach to gay men's changing relations to risk.

58. Rofes, *Dry Bones Breathe,* 129–30, summarizing a position he had staked out at greater length and in greater detail in *Reviving the Tribe,* 203–24. It may be worth observing in this connection that even the CDC at one point set a goal that stops considerably short of ending the epidemic: its HIV Prevention Strategic Plan aimed to halve the number of yearly HIV infections in the United States from forty thousand to twenty thousand. See the CDC's *HIV/AIDS Surveillance Report,* vol. 16: *Cases of HIV Infection and AIDS in the United States, 2004* (Atlanta: U.S. Department of Health and Human Services, 2005), 5.

59. Sullivan and Wolitski (note 41, above), 221–22, citing the CDC's National HIV Behavioral Surveillance survey for 2004–2005 ("HIV Prevalence, Unrecognized Infection" [note 30, above]), report a prevalence rate for HIV infection among men who have sex with men, based on a study of 1,767 MSM in five large American cities, of 25 percent overall, rising to 37 percent in the 40- to 49-year-old age group.

60. Nimmons, *Soul Beneath the Skin,* 62. Cf. Kane Race, "Plea-

sure Consuming Medicine," Ph.D. diss., University of New South Wales, 2004, 206: "But [the remarkable modification of sexual and drug practices sustained by those at risk] is not a story that we are likely to hear in contemporary publics, precisely because it would involve an account of pleasures that exceed normative forms." A revised version of this dissertation is forthcoming from Duke University Press.

61. See Sullivan and Wolitski (note 41, above), 222, 224, who survey the different studies of HIV incidence rates among various subgroups of men who have sex with men in the United States and provide a very helpful digest of the results. Note that the yearly infection rate among HIV-negative men in Sydney, an international model of HIV/AIDS prevention, is still 1 percent, according to Richters, *HIV/AIDS* (note 37, above), 3. The infection rate among gay men in San Francisco has fallen since 2001 to 1.2 percent, according to Heredia, "A Serosorting Story." No statistics of this sort can claim to be representative of the whole population of men who have sex with men: they are weighted towards those men whose participation in the social exchanges of the gay world makes them relatively accessible to researchers.

All these transmission rates are unacceptably high. "If the infection rate among HIV-negative gay men somehow were to be reduced consistently to 1 percent a year, the population of gay men in American urban centers would continue to be half infected with HIV," wrote Eric Rofes in 1996, citing a rigorous but somewhat speculative statistical study by Donald R. Hoover, Alvaro Muñoz, Vincent Carey, Joan S. Chmiel, Jeremy M. G. Taylor, Joseph B. Margolick, Lawrence Kingsley, and Sten H. Vermund, "Estimating the 1978–1990 and Future Spread of Human Immunodeficiency Virus Type 1 in Subgroups of Homosexual Men," *American Journal of Epidemiology,* 134.10 (1991): 1190–1205: see Rofes, *Reviving the Tribe,* 208. Twelve years later, Stall, "What's Driving the US Epidemic" (note 48, above), calculates that at current HIV incidence rates, which he conservatively estimates to be 2.4 percent for MSM overall and 4 percent for black MSM in the United States, HIV prevalence at age 40 is likely to be 41 percent for MSM overall and a staggering 60 percent for black MSM.

The problem, as Rofes points out, is that "once a disease has become endemic to a population . . . it requires radical interventions, such as vaccines or new technologies, to eliminate" ("Gay Bodies, Gay Selves: Understanding the Gay Men's Health Movement," *White Crane: Journal of Gay Wisdom & Culture,* 66 [Fall 2005]: 15–17, 30–34 [quotation on p. 15]). In 1998, accordingly,

Rofes called for adjusting our expectations, aiming for example to reduce the prevalence of HIV among "gay men who come of age in 2030 in epicenter cities" to 20 percent: see Rofes, *Dry Bones Breathe,* 129–30. Despite these alarming figures, Rofes properly continued to protest against the ways that epidemiological statistics are used only to blame gay men for the HIV/AIDS epidemic, never to give them credit for staying both healthy and sexually active in the midst of it (see, esp., "Gay Bodies, Gay Selves").

62. See Nimmons, *Soul Beneath the Skin,* 62, for the quip about seatbelts and heterosexual mental health. For sexual risk-taking among heterosexual youth, see Cicely Marston and Eleanor King, "Factors that Shape Young People's Sexual Behaviour: A Systematic Review," *The Lancet,* 368.9547 (November 4–10, 2006): 1581–86.

63. Mansergh et al., "Barebacking" (note 39, above), 653; also, 655, 657. Mitsch et al., "Trends in HIV/AIDS Diagnoses" (note 27, above), 683, observe that whereas the increase between 2001 and 2006 in the number of HIV/AIDS diagnoses among all black men who have sex with men was 12.4 percent in the thirty-three states with established confidential, name-based reporting (compared to 8.6 percent among MSM overall), diagnoses among black MSM aged 13–24 years increased during the same period by 93.1 percent, twice as fast as among white MSM of the same age group (and, among Asian/Pacific Islander MSM aged 13–24 years, the increase in HIV/AIDS diagnoses was 255.6 percent—though the database for this demographic group is too small to generate entirely reliable figures). The CDC now projects that in 2006 "The HIV incidence rate [in the United States as a whole] was 7 times as high among blacks (83.7; 95% CI, 70.9–96.5) as among whites (11.5; 95% CI, 9.6–13.4)": see Hall, Song, Rhodes et al., "Estimation of HIV Incidence" (note 48, above), 524.

64. David J. Malebranche, "Black Men who Have Sex with Men and the HIV Epidemic: Next Steps for Public Health," *American Journal of Public Health* 93.6 (June 2003): 862–65 (quotation on p. 862). Malebranche offers a number of possible, though speculative, solutions to this puzzle, none of which can be confirmed until more research is completed. See, further, Gregorio A. Millett, John L. Peterson, Richard J. Wolitski, and Ron Stall, "Greater Risk for HIV Infection of Black Men Who Have Sex with Men: A Critical Literature Review," *American Journal of Public Health,* 96.6 (June 2006): 1007–19, who also conclude that "high rates of infection for Black MSM . . . were not attributable to a higher frequency of risky sexual behavior" (1007). See, further, Sullivan and Wolitski (note 41, above), 228–29, and Robert E. Fullilove, *African Ameri-*

cans, Health Disparities and HIV/AIDS: Recommendations for Confronting the Epidemic in Black America (Washington, DC: National Minority AIDS Council, 2006).

65. Cf. Dean, *Beyond Sexuality*, 134n: "I focus primarily on gay men's responses to safe-sex education, not because other demographic groups remain unaffected by the issues I discuss (far from it), but because the problem is most acute for gay men and most demonstrably involves complex psychical factors." Dean goes on to provide references to work that looks at HIV/AIDS prevention as it is "differently factored by gender, race, and class." For a classic study of sexual risk-taking by gay men who belong to an ethnic minority, a study that invokes a complex set of cultural and political constraints on the agency and autonomy of these men to explain why they sometimes fail to protect themselves from infection despite their desire to do so and their clear understanding of the risks, see Rafael M. Díaz, *Latino Gay Men and HIV: Culture, Sexuality, and Risk Behavior* (New York: Routledge, 1998).

66. Tomso, "Bug Chasing" (note 24, above), 90: "What makes them do it? It seems impossible today to have a conversation about bug chasing or barebacking without hearing someone raise the question, 'What makes them do it?'" In a note, Tomso provides a bibliography of recent scholarly efforts "to catalog the reasons men engage in risky sex" (108 n. 6), to which should be added Tim Dean, "Safe Sex Education and the Death Drive," *Beyond Sexuality*, 134–73, and now Michele L. Crossley, "Making Sense of 'Barebacking': Gay Men's Narratives, Unsafe Sex and the 'Resistance Habitus,'" *British Journal of Social Psychology* 43 (2004): 225–44, and Ridge, "Incredible Thrill" (note 51, above), both discussed in a later essay by Tomso, "Risky Subjects: Public Health, Personal Narrative, and the Stakes of Qualitative Research," *Sexualities* 11.6 (2008): forthcoming. Tomso's current work provides a very useful survey as well as a wonderfully searching and subtle analysis of recent research into the subjectivity of gay male sexual risk-takers in both the scientific and the popular literature.

The most ambitious, comprehensive, and exhaustive effort to answer the question, "What makes them do it?" has now been provided by Shernoff (note 26, above), esp. 65–100, who approaches the problem from a psychological angle but who at least tries to offer a non-pathologizing solution to it.

67. For a comprehensive overview, see Ron Stall, Mark Friedman, and Joseph A. Catania, "Interacting Epidemics and Gay Men's Health: A Theory of Syndemic Production among Urban

Gay Men," in *Unequal Opportunity: Health Disparities Affecting Gay and Bisexual Men in the United States,* ed. Richard J. Wolitski, Ron Stall, and Ronald O. Valdiserri (Oxford: Oxford University Press, 2008), 251–74.

68. Stephen Lyng, ed., *Edgework: The Sociology of Risk-Taking* (New York: Routledge, 2005). The focus of the contributors to this volume is on deliberate, voluntary risk-taking, as in "extreme" sports, but the implications for our understanding of the appeal of risk are considerably wider. As Lyng points out in his introduction, "the risk experience is involved in a broader range of human endeavors than anyone might have previously imagined. . . . The studies undertaken here reveal a range of activities rooted in a common attraction to exploring the limits of human cognition and capacity in search of new possibilities of being" ("Edgework and the Risk-Taking Experience," 3–14 [quotation on p. 4]). As the late Eric Rofes, who called my attention to this book in the first place, remarked to me, the book is in some ways "the best work on barebacking of the past decade," even though "nowhere is barebacking, HIV/AIDS, or gay men's sex mentioned" (personal communication, February 11, 2006). Rofes in fact set out to explore the relevance of "edgework" to "barebacking" in a roundtable with Tony Valenzuela and Don Barrett at the annual meeting of the Pacific Sociological Association in Los Angeles on April 20–23, 2006, entitled "Risk, Thrill, and Sex without Condoms: Applying Edgework, the Sociology of Risk Taking, to Gay Men's Sex."

69. I wish to thank Marie Ymonet for emphasizing this point to me.

70. Rofes, *Reviving the Tribe,* 162.

71. I quote, with Kirk Read's kind permission, from his work in progress called *This is the Thing.* One of the few researchers to have anticipated Read's call and to be willing "to validate the negative feelings" about condoms that most gay men have is Díaz, *Latino Gay Men and HIV* (note 65, above), 15.

72. See Rofes, *Dry Bones Breathe,* esp. 198–205, for a good example of an effort to de-dramatize sexual risk-taking. Shernoff, *Without Condoms,* 267, proposes a similar strategy.

73. Lauren Berlant, "Slow Death (Sovereignty, Obesity, Lateral Agency)," *Critical Inquiry* 33.4 (Summer 2007): 754–80 (quotations on pp. 757–59).

74. See Rofes, *Reviving the Tribe,* esp. 227–82; *Dry Bones Breathe,* esp. 241–92; more recently, "Gay Bodies, Gay Selves" (note 61, above). Cf. Kippax, "A Public Health Dilemma" (note 42,

above), who makes a similar point about the current promotion of HIV testing for the purposes of prevention. And compare Sullivan and Wolitski (note 41, above), 235: "Achieving sustainable long-term gains in HIV prevention efforts for MSM may require a more holistic approach to the health and well-being of MSM. . . ."

75. Sheon and Crosby, "Ambivalent Tales" (note 35, above), 2106.

76. See Gayle S. Rubin, "The Miracle Mile: South of Market and Gay Male Leather, 1962–1997," in *Reclaiming San Francisco: History, Politics, Culture,* ed. James Brook, Chris Carlsson, and Nancy J. Peters (San Francisco: City Lights, 1998), 247–72.

77. Barry D. Adam, "Infectious Behaviour: Imputing Subjectivity to HIV Transmission," *Social Theory and Health* 4 (2006): 168–79 (quoting Barry Smart's *Economy, Culture and Society* and Deborah Lupton's *Risk* on pp. 169–70). For a similar account of how "modern systems of risk administration" create a context in which "risk rationalities" give rise to "risk identities," see Mark Davis, "HIV Prevention Rationalities and Serostatus in the Risk Narratives of Gay Men," *Sexualities* 5.3 (2002): 281–99 (also cited by Adam), esp. 285: "it flows from this system of identity production that to act in an irrational manner is deviant and, therefore, such conduct becomes a sign of defectiveness."

78. Adam, "Infectious Behaviour" (see previous note), 170, who provides plentiful references to this literature (some of the quoted phrases I have embedded in my text are from Adam himself and some are from the literature he cites, though I admit that the latter are hard to tell apart from Adam's withering rephrasings of them). The most egregious example of thirdhand, anecdotal, undocumented discussions of barebackers and bug chasers can be found in DeAnn K. Gauthier and Craig J. Forsyth, "Bareback Sex, Bug Chasers, and the Gift of Death," *Deviant Behavior* 20.1 (January 1, 1999): 85–100, an article whose complete lack of solid evidence for its sensationalistic claims has not prevented it from becoming a staple of the scholarly literature on gay men and risky sex.

For a lucid and trenchant overview of the general process of gay medical responsibilization in the United States, see Steven Epstein, "Sexualizing Governance and Medicalizing Identities: The Emergence of 'State-Centered' LGBT Health Politics in the United States," *Sexualities* 6.2 (2003): 131–71; for the United Kingdom, see Flowers, "Gay Men" (note 22, above).

79. Morales, "Persistent Pathologies" (note 2, above), 179. For a painstakingly detailed review and refutation of the scapegoating of some gay men by other gay men for allegedly lapsing from perfect

compliance with safe-sex protocols, see Rofes, *Dry Bones Breathe,* 123–97.

80. Tomso, "Bug Chasing" (note 24, above), 90. Similarly, Morales, "Persistent Pathologies," 179, who has surveyed the epidemiological literature about homosexuality and alcoholism, comments that "the end result [is] that LGBT people can never 'get well,'" and she cites the remark of a public health researcher who has done related work on ethnically motivated stigma: "Although probably not the intent of most scientists who analyze disadvantage and inequality in our society, the effects of deficits thinking can be debilitating" (Shawn Malia Kana'iaupuni, "Ka'akalai Ku Kanaka: A Call for Strengths-Based Approaches from a Native Hawaiian Perspective," *Educational Researcher,* June–July 2005, 32–38).

81. See the brilliant, eloquent, incisive, and moving essay by Tony Valenzuela, "Killer Gay Sex!" *POZ Magazine* (May 7, 2008 [web-exclusive content]; accessed August 31, 2008), http://www.poz.com/articles/killer_gay_sex_hiv_401_14539.shtml. Of course, it is the crystal methamphetamine addict and, in general, gay male abusers of illicit drugs who in recent years have served to reconsolidate the discursive connection between male homosexuality and pathology: see Race, "Pleasure Consuming Medicine" (note 60, above), chap. 6. For a genealogy of this connection, see the enlightening study by Morales, "Persistent Pathologies" (note 2, above).

82. Gregory A. Freeman, "In Search of Death," *Rolling Stone,* February 6, 2003, 44–48. For a detailed critique of this article and of the claims advanced in it, see Shernoff, *Without Condoms,* 172.

83. The study in question is by MacKellar et al., "Unrecognized HIV Infection" (note 33, above), whose sample was drawn from six U.S. cities; for the acknowledgment about upward bias, see p. 612. A 1996 investigation noted, "Whereas 90% of Australian gay men know their antibody status, US estimates place the percentage at 65% for gay men": see Coates et al., "Prevention in Developed Countries" (note 44, above), 1146, citing D. C. Berrios, N. Hearst, T. J. Coates et al., "HIV Antibody Testing among Those at Risk for Infection: The National AIDS Behavioral Surveys," *Journal of the American Medical Association* 270 (1993): 1576–80. For more recent studies, see the references in note 33, above.

84. Richard C. Friedman and Jennifer I. Downey, *Sexual Orientation and Psychoanalysis: Sexual Science and Clinical Practice* (New York: Columbia University Press, 2002).

85. Celia Kitzinger, *The Social Construction of Lesbianism* (London: Sage, 1987), 52–57.

86. Peter Hegarty, "Where's the Sex in Sexual Prejudice?" *Les-*

bian & Gay Psychology Review 7.3 (November 2006): 264–75 (quotation on p. 266).

87. Hegarty, citing Theo G. M. Sandfort, "HIV/AIDS Prevention and the Impact of Attitudes toward Homosexuality and Bisexuality," in *AIDS, Identity, and Community: The HIV Epidemic and Lesbians and Gay Men,* ed. Gregory M. Herek and Beverly Greene (Thousand Oaks, CA: Sage, 1995), 32–54.

88. That is why, despite the fact that I have a great deal of sympathy for Michele Crossley's attempt to think about gay male subjectivity as a collective phenomenon, and to emphasize its transgressive dimensions, I want to resist conceptualizing it in terms of a "cultural psyche," according to her formula ("Making Sense of Barebacking" [note 66, above]). The normalizing effects of Crossley's attempt to seek the causes of risky behavior in gay men's psyches have been vehemently criticized from *within* the field of queer psychology: see Damien W. Riggs, "Whose Morality? Constructions of 'Healthy Sexuality' in Crossley's BJSP Barebacking Paper," *Lesbian & Gay Psychology Review* 6.1 (March 2005): 45–47; Meg Barker, "Controversy in the *British Journal of Social Psychology:* A Response to Crossley," *Lesbian & Gay Psychology Review* 6.1 (March 2005): 48–52; Darren Langdridge and Paul Flowers, "Resistance Habitus and the Homophobic Social Psychologist," *Lesbian & Gay Psychology Review* 6.1 (March 2005): 53–55; and Meg Barker, Gareth Hagger-Johnson, Peter Hegarty, Craig Hutchison, and Damien Riggs, "Responses from the Lesbian & Gay Psychology Section to Crossley's 'Making Sense of "Barebacking,"'" *British Journal of Social Psychology* 46 (2007): 667–77. I do not, of course, automatically exempt work in lesbian and gay psychology from my misgivings about psychology. But the target of my critique is not social psychology, which has long demonstrated its radical possibilities, but individualizing psychology. I am also aware of the work done by queer psychologists to counteract the normalizing trends within standard academic psychological studies of gay men and lesbians.

Nor do I mean to deny that some lesbians and gay men suffer from psychological problems, or that psychological problems may play a role in the willingness of those who suffer from them to accept a degree of risk in their sexual relations. But Adam et al.'s example shows that it is possible to give an account of even individual depression in terms that are not exclusively individualizing or psychological (let alone pathological) and that moreover allow for practical ways to address the problem of HIV transmission. Thus, Adam et al. write, in reference to a man in his sixties who was infected during a period of drunken grief following the death of his partner of twenty-one years: "HIV prevention messages implicitly exhort people to act safely now in order to preserve themselves for the future. . . . To be effective, then, the prevention message calls on an autobiographical narrative that life is worth living, and that something done now makes sense because the future is a desirable place to be. . . . If life does not seem worth living now and the future appears bleak as well, then self-preserving actions no longer make sense" ("AIDS Optimism" [note 25, above], 241–42). This recalls the observation made by Donna M. Orange, "High-Risk Behavior or High-Risk Systems? Discussion of Cheuvront's 'High-Risk Sexual Behavior in the Treatment of HIV-Negative Patients,'" *Journal of Gay & Lesbian Psychotherapy* 6.3 (2002): 45–50: "the conceptual problem here is that risk-taking is not a 'behavior' at all, but a property of a relational system" (48, quoted and cited by Tomso, "Bug Chasing," 103). See also Suarez and Miller, "Negotiating Risks in Context" (note 26, above); Davis, "HIV Prevention Rationalities" (note 77, above); Hodges and Rodohan (note 28, above); Díaz, *Latino Gay Men and HIV* (note 65, above), 53–54; and Gilbert Émond, "Processus de séduction et protection contre le VIH dans l'expérience sexuelle des hommes gais de Montréal," Ph.D. diss., Université du Québec à Montréal, 2005; all of whom emphasize the importance of context and relationality.

Kane Race bears out that claim by providing a brilliant, non-psychological account of the challenges facing prevention efforts in the era of antiretroviral therapies and the privatization of HIV/AIDS: see chapter 5 of "Pleasure Consuming Medicine" (note 60, above), an earlier version of which appeared in the form of an important article, "The Undetectable Crisis: Changing Technologies of Risk," *Sexualities* 4 (2001): 167–89.

89. Michael Warner, "Unsafe: Why Gay Men Are Having Risky Sex," *Village Voice,* January 31, 1995, 32–36. All further page references to this article will be incorporated in the text.

90. Public Health Watch, *HIV/AIDS Policy in the United States: Monitoring the UNGASS Declaration of Commitment on HIV/AIDS. A series of reports on HIV/AIDS policy in Nicaragua, Senegal, Ukraine, the United States, Vietnam, and Zambia* (New York: Open Society Institute, 2006), 24. Even the CDC has indicated that only 55 percent of people living with HIV/AIDS in the United States who needed antiretroviral therapy received it in 2005, in contrast to 83 percent of HIV-infected persons in Brazil: see "The Global HIV/AIDS Pandemic" (above, note 48), 842. Harold Jaffe, a lead-

ing HIV/AIDS researcher and former Director of the National Center for HIV, STD, and TB Prevention at the CDC, in a plenary address entitled "Status of the US HIV/AIDS Epidemic: Is It Changing and If Not, Why Not?", delivered at the Fourteenth Conference on Retroviruses and Opportunistic Infections in Los Angeles, on February 27, 2007, noted that the current mortality rate from HIV/AIDS in the United States (seventeen thousand in 2005, or about 58 per million of population) is twice that of any country in the European Union and ten times that in the United Kingdom.

91. See, for example, Greg Behrman, *The Invisible People: How the U.S. Has Slept through the Global AIDS Pandemic, the Greatest Humanitarian Catastrophe of our Time* (New York: Free Press, 2004).

92. For the CDC's latest, revised calculations, see Hall, Song, Rhodes et al., "Estimation of HIV Incidence" (note 48, above), esp. 525, and *Estimates of New HIV Infections in the United States* (note 48, above). The most recent yearly estimate has a confidence interval of 95 percent, which allows for a fairly wide margin of error: thus, the figure of 56,300 new infections in 2006 actually represents a possible range from 48,200 to 64,500.

93. See, generally, Cindy Patton, *Fatal Advice: How Safe Sex Education Went Wrong* (Durham, NC: Duke University Press, 1996). I do not mean to imply that there are no local variations in prevention paradigms or that U.S. standards of HIV/AIDS prevention are monolithic.

Eric Rofes has argued, further, that the policy of risk elimination and the ethic of perfect compliance with safe-sex guidelines can boomerang by making unsafe sex seem transgressive and therefore appealing: for the most recent version of this argument, see Eric Rofes, *A Radical Rethinking of Sexuality and Schooling: Status Quo or Status Queer?* (Lanham, MD: Rowman & Littlefield, 2005), 121–33. (See also Suarez and Miller, "Negotiating Risks in Context," 294; Shernoff, *Without Condoms,* 33.) I agree, and I think this is a crucial consideration, but because it is not central to Warner's argument, I have not highlighted it in my analysis here.

94. Cf. Walt Odets, *In the Shadow of the Epidemic: Being HIV-Negative in the Age of AIDS* (Durham, NC: Duke University Press, 1995), 39.

95. However, Barry D. Adam, Winston Husbands, James Murray, and John Maxwell, *Renewing HIV Prevention for Gay and Bisexual Men: A Research Report on Safer Sex Practices Among High-Risk Men and Men in Couples in Toronto,* A Report to Health Canada (2003), 32, warn that "'risk reduction' messages" may "ultimately

affirm the 'boundary pushing' practices of some men, and indeed may help consolidate such practices as viable forms of risk reduction." In this way, they observe, some harm reduction strategies may "simply function[ ] as a cover for harm increase." For a detailed and subtle analysis that supports this point, with specific reference to the Australian model, see Juliet Richters, Olympia Hendry, and Susan Kippax, "When Safe Sex Isn't Safe," *Culture, Health & Sexuality* 5.1 (2003): 37–52. For a careful and nuanced assessment of risk reduction messages and their effects, see Sean Slavin, Juliet Richters, and Susan Kippax, "Understandings of Risk among HIV Seroconverters in Sydney," *Health, Risk & Society* 6.1 (March 2004): 39–52. This research offers an important corrective to similar but cruder epidemiological critiques of risk reduction practices, such as the otherwise valuable overview offered by Richard J. Wolitski and Bernard M. Branson, "'Grey Area Behaviors' and Partner Selection Strategies: Working Toward a Comprehensive Approach to Reducing the Sexual Transmission of HIV," in *Beyond Condoms: Alternative Approaches to HIV Prevention,* ed. Ann O'Leary (New York: Kluwer Academic/Plenum, 2002), 173–98.

96. There are local variations in HIV/AIDS prevention strategies in the United States, and some combination of risk elimination with risk reduction does occur. For a critical discussion of some rare examples, see Rofes, *Dry Bones Breathe,* 234–36, and *Radical Rethinking,* 129–32.

97. Adam et al., *Renewing HIV Prevention* (note 95, above), 1 (citing five studies from the end of the 1990s) and 29; Adam et al., "AIDS Optimism" (note 25, above), 238; Elford, "Changing Patterns" (note 28, above) 27, citing five recent studies; Parsons et al., "Correlates of Risk Behaviors" (note 22, above), 384, citing a variety of studies that give reason for concern about current HIV transmission rates; similarly, Wolitski, "The Emergence of Barebacking," 10–11 (note 33, above); Beryl Koblin, Margaret Chesney, Thomas Coates, Kenneth Mayer et al., "Effects of a Behavioural Intervention to Reduce Acquisition of HIV Infection among Men Who Have Sex with Men: The EXPLORE Randomised Controlled Study," *The Lancet,* 364.9428 (3–9 July 2004), 41–50. For the increase in name-based HIV/AIDS diagnoses from 2003 to 2006, and the stability in the estimated numbers of newly diagnosed cases of AIDS in the United States as a whole, see the CDC's *HIV/AIDS Surveillance Report* for 2006 (note 21, above), 11 and 13 (tables 1 and 3), along with my discussion of these statistics in note 27.

98. Rofes, *Reviving the Tribe,* 198, offers the following description of an article by Michelangelo Signorile, "Negative Pride," pub-

lished in *Out* magazine several months later, in March 1995, but I believe his words apply more aptly to Warner's earlier essay, even if Warner was talking about risk-taking rather than seroconversion: "the first mass media account of new seroconversions which begins to confront difficult ethical questions head on and shares responsibility for new infections with both the previously uninfected man as well as the infected man."

99. Odets, *Shadow of the Epidemic* (note 94, above), 257, 218.

100. See Jesse Green, "Flirting With Suicide," *New York Times Magazine,* September 15, 1996, 39–45, 54–55, 84–85, esp. 43.

101. Paul Willis, *Learning to Labor* (New York: Columbia University Press, 1977), 34, as quoted and cited by Stephen Lyng, "Sociology at the Edge: Social Theory and Voluntary Risk Taking," *Edgework* (note 68, above), 17–49 (quotation on p. 20). Willis was in fact referring to street fighting among juvenile delinquents in the United Kingdom.

102. Berlant, "Slow Death" (note 73, above), 779–80. On futurity as the basis of all politics and all morality, see Lee Edelman, *No Future: Queer Theory and the Death Drive* (Durham, NC: Duke University Press, 2004).

103. For Australia, see Rosengarten, Race, and Kippax, *Touch Wood* (note 43, above); Kippax and Race, "Sustaining Safe Practice: Twenty Years On" (note 43, above); Race, "Revaluation of Risk among Gay Men" (note 39, above), citing an abundance of secondary literature; and Paul Van de Ven, Limin Mao, Andrea Fogarty, Patrick Rawstorne, June Crawford, Garrett Prestage, Andrew Grulich, John Kaldor, and Susan Kippax, "Undetectable Viral Load Is Associated with Sexual Risk Taking in HIV Serodiscordant Gay Couples in Sydney," *AIDS* 19.2 (January 28, 2005): 179–84. For Canada, see Adam et al., *Renewing HIV Prevention* (note 95, above). For the United States, see Parsons et al., "Correlates of Risk Behaviors" (note 22, above). U.S. data collection tends to favor quantitative over qualitative information-gathering, but see the Positive Partners Study in San Francisco that documents serosorting (Heredia, "A Serosorting Story"); also, Díaz, *Latino Gay Men and HIV* (note 65, above), whose combination of quantitative and qualitative research foregrounds collective experiences of subjectivity.

104. See Rosengarten, Race, and Kippax, *Touch Wood.* Adam et al., *Renewing HIV Prevention,* esp. 21–32, confirm this picture and fill in a number of additional details, though they also present evidence that some risk reduction strategies that gay men have been using may not in fact be effective, and may be responsible for an increase in new HIV infections (6–8); they also document the

prevalence of "stupidity" as a factor in some gay men's sexual risk-taking, even according to the criteria of the gay risk-takers themselves (11). (On this perennially neglected consideration, see, generally, Avital Ronell, *Stupidity* [Urbana: University of Illinois Press, 2002].) For a more accessible recapitulation of this study, see now Adam et al., "AIDS Optimism" (note 25, above).

105. For the documentation of a specific example, see Paul Flowers, Barbara Duncan, and Jamie Frankis, "Community, Responsibility and Culpability: HIV Risk-Management amongst Scottish Gay Men," *Journal of Community & Applied Social Psychology* 10 (2000): 285–300: "Several of the negative and untested men believed that HIV positive people should bear a greater responsibility in managing HIV risk-reduction during sexual activity with negative or untested men. . . . In contrast, HIV positive participants tended to highlight the responsibility of each individual to manage their own health" (292–93, 295), though the interview data presented clearly shows that some HIV-positive individuals considered that it was their responsibility to protect their sexual partners. Less helpful, though more recent, is the statistical study by Trevor A. Hart, Richard J. Wolitski, David W. Purcell, Jeffrey T. Parsons, Cynthia A. Gómez, and the Seropositive Urban Men's Study Team, "Partner Awareness of the Serostatus of HIV-Seropositive Men Who Have Sex With Men: Impact on Unprotected Sexual Behavior," *AIDS and Behavior* 9.2 (June 2005): 155–66.

See, further, Davis, "HIV Prevention Rationalities" (note 77, above), 289–92; Adam et al., *Renewing HIV Prevention* (note 95, above), 31–32, who speak of "semiotic snares" and "self-negating prescriptions," noting that "HIV is an opportunistic illness of the predominant discourses of our era just as it is of immune systems" (2). Adam et al., "AIDS Optimism" (note 25, above), 246–47, recapitulating those points, note the existence of prevention campaigns in San Francisco and Toronto designed specifically to call to the attention of men who have sex with men the dangers of making too many tacit assumptions about a partner's HIV-status on the basis of his decision not to use a condom. Suarez and Miller (note 26, above), 292–93, include such tacit assumptions in their category of "irrational" risk-taking, but I would argue that not all "faulty heuristics used to gauge risk" (293) should be considered *irrational* merely because they are *faulty*.

106. See Race, "Culture of Barebacking" (note 32, above); Sheon and Crosby, "Ambivalent Tales" (note 35, above); Hodges and Rodohan, "Living with Homophobia" (note 28, above).

107. Race, "Pleasure Consuming Medicine" (note 60, above),

218–19. Race goes on to qualify his account as follows: "Upon the identification of the workings of medicine in gay sex, the field of HIV prevention in Australia became prolific with accounts of 'sophisticated gay men making complex decisions to reduce risk.' At times, these descriptions seemed to verge on a populist romanticism that celebrated every instance of gay men's appropriation of medicine as though it were inherently safe. We heard a lot about gay men's 'cultures of care,' for example, but comparatively little was offered in the way of empirical analysis of the shape of these cultures, or the practices of differentiation that went into ensuring care, or their concrete effects. Often one was left with the impression that all gay educators needed to do was provide a few scientific facts, trust gay men, and put all stock in lived cultures that were inherently resistant, subversive, communal, sophisticated, and safe. To some extent, these problems are inherent in the theories of everyday life upon which these analyses more or less explicitly draw. The excess of process over structure is often regarded as a cause for political celebration in itself, with little concern for how, concretely, such excess reworks the social field. But applied to the field of HIV prevention, these impressions become as good an argument as any for justifying the appalling shortfalls that currently threaten to wind down education and research in the field of gay men's health promotion. After all, if gay culture is inherently well informed and productive of non-problematic cultures of care, there is not much left for health educators to do. It seems to me that the reason for attending to embodied agency in the field of health promotion is not simply to celebrate the endlessly inventive practices of everyday life or sex (though well we might). It is to provide much needed information about the cultural conditions in which particular dangers and possibilities—both social and physical—take shape. Some of these possibilities arise from the very practices of differentiation that are adopted to promote safety (such as those that discriminate between HIV-positive or HIV-negative sexual partners . . .). Health promoters need to monitor the cultural effects of these practices carefully and, when problematic, respond to them" (219–20).

This echoes the cautionary point made by Adam et al., *Renewing HIV Prevention,* 32, and "AIDS Optimism," 240–41, about the way some harm reduction strategies may function as a cover for harm increase (see note 95, above). Stall, "What's Driving the US Epidemic" (note 48, above), makes the crucial point that no studies have been done to determine whether risk reduction strategies actually work or to measure just how much or how little they reduce risk, if indeed they do.

108. Race, "Culture of Barebacking" (note 32, above). For some examples of the research that Race is summarizing here, see Mansergh et al., "Barebacking" (note 39, above), 656: "The reason most frequently cited for barebacking was to experience greater physical stimulation; feeling emotionally connected with a partner was also a relatively common reason"; also, Adam et al., *Renewing HIV Prevention* (note 95, above), who conclude on the basis of a more extensive qualitative study: "Unprotected sex arises in a variety of disparate circumstances: as a resolution to . . . erectile difficulties [caused by the use of condoms], through momentary lapses and trade offs, out of personal turmoil and depression, and as a byproduct of strategies of disclosure and intuiting safety. It is also strongly associated with relationship development and the communication of trust and intimacy. In addition, the development of a culture of unprotected sex among a subset of urban HIV-positive men poses further challenges in crafting adequate HIV prevention programming. There is no 'average' gay man nor 'average' factor determining unsafe sex" (30).

109. Berlant, "Slow Death" (note 73, above), 777, note 60 and 757–58.

110. For example, even Mansergh et al., "Barebacking" (note 39, above), observe that of the small number of HIV-negative men in this San Francisco sample who deliberately barebacked 17 percent gave as their reasons "to do something taboo or racy" and 22 percent "to take a major risk" (p. 657, table 2). Ridge, "Incredible Thrill" (note 51, above), 266, provides additional confirmation of such motives for barebacking. Furthermore, the conclusion of Adam et al., *Renewing HIV Prevention,* quoted in note 108, above, is based directly on empirical research among gay and bisexual men in Toronto, though it also takes into account findings from similar research in other parts of the world, whereas Warner was attempting to convey the cultural climate of gay men in New York at a particular moment. Moreover, as Adam and others admit (for some direct quotations, see note 158, below), it is not in the nature of qualitative research to establish ultimate motives for behavior. In this case, it is not likely that interview data could ever confirm or deny some of Warner's more speculative hypotheses.

111. Michele Crossley speaks, in similar terms, of a "resistance habitus" on the part of gay men ("Making Sense of Barebacking" [note 66, above], 237–39); see also Shernoff, *Without Condoms,* 92–94. Some studies do find a correlation among "esoteric" sex (which may be experienced as transgressive, though it is not necessarily risky in itself), barebacking, and seroconversion: for an

overview, see Susan Kippax et al., "Cultures of Sexual Adventurism as Markers of HIV Seroconversion: A Case Control Study in a Cohort of Sydney Gay Men," *AIDS Care* 10.6 (1998): 677–88; Gary Smith, Heather Worth, and Susan Kippax, *Sexual Adventurism among Sydney Gay Men,* National Centre in HIV Social Research, Monograph 3/2004 (Sydney: National Centre in HIV Social Research, 2004). Barry Adam (personal communication, February 7, 2006) reports similar findings in the Toronto Pride Survey.

Eric Rofes speculates that gay men's habit of transgression may explain why safe sex campaigns that attempt to make us into better citizens tend to backfire and produce the opposite result, rendering the prohibited attractive. He asks, "If resistance to health promotion is deeply rooted in the sexual subjectivities of a large portion of gay men—and if this resistance is linked to our production of ourselves as gender-nonconforming, sexual outlaws—will *any* form of health promotion serve to improve the health and wellness of gay men?" (*Radical Rethinking* [note 93, above], 133).

112. For a similar approach to questions of consciousness in gay men's motivation for unsafe sex, see Crossley, "Making Sense of Barebacking," 227–28, who, despite a certain uneasiness with psychoanalysis, opts for a psychological rather than, say, an ethical model of explanation.

113. Tim Dean, however, criticizes Crimp for not going far enough, accusing him of conceptualizing the death drive in what still remain pop-psychological terms: see *Beyond Sexuality,* 119–20.

114. I quote Foucault's long-unpublished 1978 interview with Jean Le Bitoux, "Le gay savoir," most recently printed in Le Bitoux, *Entretiens sur la question gay* (Béziers: H&O, 2005), 45–72 (quotation on p. 50).

115. Recent ethnographic work on seroconversion, however, indicates that Warner's understanding of his experience of unsafe sex in terms of being overwhelmed by irrational impulses may not be typical, at least not in the comparatively secular world of contemporary Australia: see Slavin, Richters, and Kippax, "Understandings of Risk" (note 95, above). However, the insistence of recent seroconverters in Sydney on their own rationality and ability to exercise choice may indicate the extent to which they have bought into a neoliberal, voluntarist conception of responsible citizenship, itself an effect of certain kinds of HIV prevention rhetoric, as Race has now argued in "Culture of Barebacking."

116. Dean, *Beyond Sexuality,* 136.

117. For a brilliant demonstration of this point, see Paul Morri-

son, *The Explanation for Everything: Essays on Sexual Subjectivity* (New York: New York University Press, 2001).

118. Dean, *Beyond Sexuality,* 132, 122. To be sure, Dean does emphasize that "sexual antagonism is . . . internal to every person as an effect of every subject's constitutive *sexual* dependence upon the Other" (128), that "the death drive inhabits our being" (133), and that "in a psychotic society we are all PWAs" (132), thereby insisting that the death drive is part of our incurable human condition, not the unique property of white gay men. Even so, by taking HIV/AIDS as "a figure for death in life" (133), he describes a contemporary social situation in such a way that the death drive acquires a particular pertinence to those infected with HIV and, by extension, to gay men in general. And, in fact, we are *not* all people living with HIV/AIDS, psychotic society or no; for those who are not infected with HIV to pretend or boast that they are does little for the cause of solidarity between HIV-positive and HIV-negative folks: people living with HIV/AIDS get little enough attention and few enough resources as it is.

119. Julia Kristeva, *Pouvoirs de l'horreur. Essai sur l'abjection* (Paris: Seuil, 1980).

120. See Didier Eribon, *Insult and the Making of the Gay Self,* trans. Michael Lucey (Durham, NC: Duke University Press, 2004).

121. Alberto Sladogna has kindly provided me with a list of the occurrences of *abjection* in Lacan's published texts and seminars. In the *Écrits* (Paris: Seuil, 1966), see "Le séminaire sur 'la Lettre volée'" (54); "Propos sur la causalité psychique" (170); "La direction de la cure et les principes de son pouvoir" (638); "Remarque sur le rapport de Daniel Lagache: 'Psychanalyse et structure de la personnalité'" (664); and "Subversion du sujet et dialectique du désir dans l'inconscient freudien" (803). In none of those instances does *abjection* qualify as a technical term; on the contrary, it is used mostly to refer to the intellectual poverty of contemporary psychoanalysis. In the third of Lacan's televised interviews, where Lacan compares the psychoanalyst to the saint, the term *abjection* appears in passing but seems to bear little theoretical weight: Jacques Lacan, *Télévision* (Paris: Éditions du Seuil, 1973), 28. For uses of "abjection" in the seminars, see "L'étique de la psychanalyse," session of March 30, 1960; "La logique du fantasme," session of April 19, 1967; "Ou pire," session of June 21, 1972; "Encore," session of May 8, 1973; "Les non-dupes errent," session of November 20, 1973.

122. Jean-Paul Sartre, *Saint Genet. Comédien et martyr* (Paris: Gallimard, 1952). Kristeva does not explicitly engage with Sartre,

nor does she mention Genet, but she dismisses Sartre's book allusively by devoting a third of her book to Céline, whom she calls in the title of one of her chapters "ni comédien ni martyr."

123. See Sartre, *Saint Genet,* and Didier Eribon, *Une morale du minoritaire. Variations sur un thème de Jean Genet* (Paris: Fayard, 2001), esp. 69–136, to whom I owe this entire genealogy of abjection. For a more extended consideration of Jouhandeau, see Didier Eribon, "L'abjecté abjecteur. Quelques remarques sur l'antisémitisme gay des années 1930 à nos jours," *Hérésies. Essais sur la théorie de la sexualité* (Paris: Fayard, 2003), 169–206, esp. 175–88.

124. Marcel Jouhandeau, *De l'abjection* (Nantes: Le Passeur-Cecofop, 1999 [orig. publ. Paris: Gallimard, 1939]), 17. Further page references will be incorporated in the text; I am responsible for all the English-language quotations.

125. Jean Genet, *Journal du voleur* (1949; Paris: Folio, 2001), 237: "Si la sainteté est mon but . . ." On this general theme, see the extended discussion in Sartre, *Saint Genet,* 220–81.

126. Sartre, *Saint Genet,* 104. Cf. p. 19: "Dans le mysticisme de Genet on discerne . . . un refus de l'ordre humain."

127. Jean Genet, *Miracle de la rose* (Décines [Rhône]: L'Arbalète, 1946; rpt. 1993), 314–15: "Si l'habituelle sainteté consiste à monter dans un ciel vers son idole, la sainteté qui me menait vers Harcamone en étant exactement le contraire, il était normal que les exercices m'y conduisant fussent d'un autre ordre que les exercices qui mènent au ciel. Je devais aller à lui par un autre chemin que celui de la vertu. . . . L'abjection où se tenait Divers—et celle, plus intense, de nos deux volontés réunies—nous enfonçaient la tête en bas, à l'opposé du ciel, dans le ténèbres. . . . L'influence d'Harcamone agissait vraiment selon sa parfaite destination : par lui, notre âme était ouverte à l'extrême abjection. Il faut bien que j'emploie la terminologie imagée dont on se sert couramment. Qu'on ne s'étonne pas si les images qui indiquent mon mouvement sont l'opposé des images qui indiquent le mouvement des saints du ciel. On dira d'eux qu'ils montaient, et que je me dégradais. . . . Les voies de la sainteté sont étroites, c'est-à-dire qu'il est impossible de les éviter et lorsque, par malheur, on s'y est engagé, de s'y retourner pour revenir en arrière. On est saint par la force des choses qui est la force de Dieu !" Further page references will be incorporated in the text; I am responsible for all the English-language quotations.

Eribon, *Une morale du minoritaire,* 69, commenting on Genet's *Thief's Journal,* succinctly defines abjection as the loss of humanity that a human being suffers through being relegated to the status of a pariah by the gaze of those who are socially dominant.

128. Sartre, *Saint Genet,* 156, 268.

129. For a similar effort to imagine how social degradation might give rise to community among the shamed, see the beautiful essay by Douglas Crimp, "Mario Montez, For Shame," in *Regarding Sedgwick: Essays on Queer Culture and Critical Theory,* ed. Stephen M. Barber and David L. Clark (New York: Routledge, 2002), 57–70.

130. Cf. James Hillman, *The Myth of Analysis: Three Essays in Archetypal Psychology* (1960; rpt. Evanston, IL: Northwestern University Press, 1999), 146.

131. For a similar analysis of working-class criminality as a response to shame and social humiliation—a way of trying to scare off humiliation, to run "along the edge of shame for its exciting reverberations"—see Jack Katz, *Seductions of Crime: Moral and Sensual Attractions in Doing Evil* (New York: Basic Books, 1988), 312–13, cited by Lyng, "Sociology at the Edge," 28. The same passage from Katz is quoted in a similar context by Tony Valenzuela in his contribution to Eric Rofes's roundtable (see note 68, above).

132. My formulation here borrows from Leo Bersani's account of masochism in *Homos* (Cambridge: Harvard University Press, 1995), 99.

133. Sartre, *Saint Genet,* 143–44. Sartre continues to argue against an exclusively psychoanalytic interpretation throughout *Saint Genet:* see, for example, pp. 180, 645.

134. Michel Foucault, *Madness and Civilization: A History of Insanity in the Age of Reason,* trans. Richard Howard (New York: Pantheon, 1965), x–xi.

135. This interpretation originates with Sartre, not with me: see *Saint Genet,* 648–50.

136. This reversal is of course the major theme of Sartre's *Saint Genet.*

137. Genet, *Journal du voleur,* 237 (quoted with commentary by Eribon, *Une morale du minoritaire,* 102). See also p. 100 for a similar sentiment.

138. These two scenes are consistently discussed together by Sartre, who groups them under the rubric "miracles of horror": see, for example, *Saint Genet,* 306, 348. Eribon, *Une morale du minoritaire,* 106–9, also treats these two passages in Genet in close proximity, for similar reasons, but he is more concerned with the concept than with the actual vocabulary of abjection. For some extended readings of the scene from *Journal du voleur,* which pursue different topics from mine, see Sartre, *Saint Genet,* 539–48; Dick Hebdige, "Introduction: Subculture and Style," *Subculture: The*

Meaning of Style (London: Routledge, 1979), 1–4; Éric Marty, *Jean Genet, post-scriptum. Essai* (Lagasse: Verdier, 2006), 25ff; John Plotz, "Objects of Abjection: The Animation of Difference in Jean Genet's Novels," *Twentieth Century Literature,* 44.1 (Spring 1998): 100–118.

139. Genet, *Journal du voleur,* 20. I quote the excellent English translation by Bernard Frechtman (which is based on the original, unexpurgated edition of Genet's text, never reprinted and still unavailable in France or anywhere else), to which I have made a number of adjustments: Jean Genet, *The Thief's Journal,* trans. Bernard Frechtman (New York: Grove Press, 1964), 19.

140. Genet, *Journal du voleur,* 20–23; Genet, *The Thief's Journal,* 19–22. I have written "Adoration of the Magi" where Genet has "Perpetual Adoration" (referring to the veneration of the Blessed Sacrament of the Eucharist), as I think the former image will be more evocative for an English-speaking audience unfamiliar with the details of Catholic spirituality.

141. Genet, *Journal du voleur,* 23; Genet, *The Thief's Journal,* 22.

142. E.g., Genet, *Journal du voleur,* 29.

143. See Foucault, "Le gay savoir," 51.

144. For more on agency and the subject along these lines, see Judith Butler, "Contingent Foundations: Feminism and the Question of 'Postmodernism,'" in *Feminists Theorize the Political,* ed. Judith Butler and Joan W. Scott (New York: Routledge, 1992), 3–21.

145. Berlant, "Slow Death," 759.

146. I take it that this is precisely what Leo Bersani denies in *Homos,* 77–97. In his earlier essay, "Is the Rectum a Grave?" in *AIDS: Cultural Analysis/Cultural Activism,* ed. Douglas Crimp = *October* 43 (Winter 1987): 197–222, however, Bersani distinguished more carefully between the death of "the self" and "biological death" (222).

147. Psychoanalytic critics may object that I fail here to distinguish between pleasure and *jouissance.* See Tim Dean, "Sex and Syncope," *Raritan* 15.3 (Winter 1996): 64–86, esp. 85–86, for precisely this objection. I consider the distinction a conceptually useful one in certain contexts, but it is sometimes hard to apply in practice, and it should not be mistaken for an airtight division or a theoretical truth.

148. I owe this insight to my discussions with Brent Armendinger.

149. Hervé Guibert, *À l'ami qui ne m'a pas sauvé la vie* (Paris: Gallimard, 1990), 242; cf. *To the Friend Who Did Not Save My Life,*

trans. Linda Coverdale (New York: Scribner, 1991), 223. I quote the more accurate translation provided by Lee Edelman, who also supplies a brilliant discussion of the passage, in "The Mirror and the Tank: 'AIDS,' Subjectivity, and the Rhetoric of Activism," *Homographesis: Essays in Gay Literary and Cultural Theory* (New York: Routledge, 1994), 93–117, esp. 115–16 (quotation on p. 116).

150. Race, "Culture of Barebacking," citing Scott O'Hara, *Autopornography: A Memoir of Life in the Lust Lane* (New York: Harrington Park Press, 1997), 129.

151. Compare Genet's line, "J'ai décidé d'être ce que le crime a fait de moi," which Sartre uses as the title of part 2, chapter 2, of *Saint Genet*.

152. I thank Greg Tomso for making this point to me.

153. For some documented examples of this phenomenon, see Shernoff, *Without Condoms*, 162–63. See, now, Tim Dean, "Breeding Culture: Barebacking, Bugchasing, Giftgiving," *Massachusetts Review*, 49.1–2 (Spring/Summer 2008): 80–94, who takes the fantasy literally.

154. See, for example, Sheon and Crosby, "Ambivalent Tales"; Hodges and Rodohan, "Living with Homophobia."

155. Brent Armendinger, personal communication, February 8, 2006.

156. Tomso, "Bug Chasing," 102.

157. In *Beyond Sexuality*, Tim Dean attempts to get around this problem by insisting that the unconscious is also social, with specific reference to what he (following Lacan) calls the Symbolic. "Before going any further" in connecting the difficulties of HIV/AIDS prevention with the death drive, he is careful to maintain, "I should reemphasize that I understand the unconscious to be an effect of the symbolic order—a precipitate of those networks of signifiers that are culturally determined but also always inflected by subjective particularities. Thinking about AIDS in terms of the symbolic order rather than in terms of individual risk promises to illuminate how social fantasies about erotic *jouissance* guarantee safe-sex education's failure" (136). In this effort to move the analysis of sexual practice away from questions of individual risk and towards a consideration of collective or social vicissitudes, Dean's project is very much in line with my own (though I reject the claim that HIV/AIDS prevention has failed or is guaranteed to fail). But it is very hard to see how the Symbolic in Dean's formulation differs from the circulation of social meanings that are taken up in social psychology. In fact, despite his insistence on the distinction between psychology and psychoanalysis, Dean cannot seem to resist

psychologizing his own theory. Although he insists that "the concept of the death drive is perhaps the one that most clearly distinguishes psychoanalysis from psychology, for the death drive is reducible neither to the level of consciousness or the unconscious, nor to the popular notion of self-destructiveness that has been leveled at gay men with renewed homophobic vigor in the wake of AIDS" (120), he nonetheless invokes the death drive to explain the conscious, explicit statements of gay male subjects about their psychological motivations for engaging in sexual practices that carry a potential risk of transmitting HIV. In other words, behaviors that are characterized by the subjects themselves as self-destructive are cited by Dean as symptoms of the death drive. Dean's critical practice transforms the death drive from a psychoanalytic concept to a psychological one. And that simply reproduces the popular notion about gay men's pathological self-destructiveness that Dean claims to be arguing against.

158. Adam et al., "AIDS Optimism" (note 25, above), 245, adding, in reference to HIV-positive men, "No one in this study expressed willingness or acceptance of the idea of knowingly infecting a partner." (See, also, Shernoff, *Without Condoms,* 175–76.) But in another article, Adam et al. properly caution that "discourses about personal practice cannot be taken simply as a direct reflection of motivation or a straightforward record of 'what happened.' . . . [N]either discourse analysis nor more positive research methodologies offer direct access to behaviour or motivation" ("Risk Construction" [note 43, above], 64). Crossley, "Making Sense of Barebacking" (note 66, above), 226–27, expresses specific reservations about the use of interview data from gay men in the context of HIV/AIDS prevention. See, further, Tomso, "Risky Subjects" (note 66, above).

159. Douglas Crimp, "How to Have Promiscuity in an Epidemic," in Crimp, ed., *AIDS: Cultural Analysis/Cultural Activism = October* 43 (Winter 1987): 237–71, esp. 253; see the detailed discussion of this point by Lauren Berlant and Michael Warner, "Sex in Public," *Critical Inquiry* 24.2 (Winter 1998): 547–66, esp. 560–61. For a telling example of psychoanalytic antagonism to Crimp's argument, see Dean, *Beyond Sexuality,* 128–31.

160. Berlant, "Slow Death," 779.

161. For a broad survey of these developments, see Rofes, *Dry Bones Breathe.*

162. Dean, "Sex and Syncope" (note 147, above), 75. Dean compounds this misjudgment by denying the very possibility of safe sex. In *Beyond Sexuality,* he claims that sex itself is unsafe because "the

capacity inherent in sexual *jouissance* to undo the coherent self means that there is something *psychically* dangerous about sex as such. . . . Indeed, once sexuality is understood in terms of what shatters the self, then the very notion of safe sex becomes oxymoronic" (164; Dean's italics). Although Dean goes on to acknowledge that "from the perspective of AIDS education, it is imperative to distinguish what's *psychically* dangerous from what's *physically* dangerous," he believes that that is "a difficult distinction to maintain when one is engaged in a [*sic*] encounter that is, after all, always physical" (165). No doubt—but the slide from the psychic to the physical via the concrete act of sex in this formulation is simplistic and evasive. Dean is surely right to "appreciate the fantasmatic significance of overriding latex barriers in sex" (164), but if *sexuality itself*, by its very nature or the nature of its *jouissance,* is "inassimilable to the self," psychically dangerous (164), and intolerable by reason of "one's 'own' excess *jouissance* in the Other" (139), and if, as Dean claims, all this is true of all human sexuality, howsoever it is "acted out" through sexual contact, then sex will be "unsafe" whether or not you wear a condom. In which case, you might as well wear one. In other words, there is no connection, even on Dean's account, between the alleged psychic unsafeness of sex in itself and particular sexual acts that carry a risk of transmitting HIV.

163. For an example, see Díaz, *Latino Gay Men and HIV,* 137–75, whose psychological model has been informed by empirical social analysis and adapted to fit a particular cultural situation. In this case, the theory emerges from a locally based, site-specific study and generates an activist intervention that is locally focused and context-specific.

164. For an exception to this tendency, and an eloquent protest against it, see Biddy Martin, "Sexualities without Genders and other Queer Utopias," *diacritics* 24.2–3 (Summer/Autumn 1994): 104–21, rpt. in Martin, *Femininity Played Straight* (note 1, above), 71–94.

165. For a survey of different approaches to the politics of the subject, see Adam, "Domination, Resistance, and Subjectivity" (note 6, above).

166. For a particularly dystopian reading of Genet, by way of alternative to the reading offered here, see Bersani, *Homos,* 151–81.

167. Foucault, *L'Herméneutique du sujet,* 241; *Hermeneutics of the Subject,* 251–52. I have taken the liberty of altering somewhat the published translation.

168. See Eribon, *Une morale du minoritaire,* 67–68, 105n, 109, 134. In a different but related context, Wendy Brown writes,

"Deities, angels, specters, and ghosts . . . what are we to make of these creatures rising from the pens of radical thinkers in the twentieth century as they attempt to grasp our relation to the past and future, and in particular as they attempt to articulate the prospects for a postfoundational formulation of justice?" See Brown, "Specters and Angels: Benjamin and Derrida," *Politics Out Of History* (Princeton: Princeton University Press, 2001), 138–73 (quotation on pp. 142–43).

169. That is precisely what is fatally unqueer about politics, according to Lee Edelman in *No Future.* It will be clear that my own approach departs sharply from Edelman's, despite my admiration for his uncompromisingly radical and radically uncompromising position. For alternate models, see Eve Kosofsky Sedgwick, "Epidemics of the Will," in *Tendencies* (Durham, NC: Duke University Press, 1993), 130–42, who speaks of "habit" as "a version of repeated action that moves, not toward metaphysical absolutes, but toward interrelations of the action—and the self acting—with the bodily habitus, the appareling habit, the sheltering habitation, everything that marks the traces of that habit on a world that the metaphysical absolutes would have left a vacuum" (138), adding, "It is extraordinarily difficult to imagine an analytically usable language of habit, in a conceptual landscape so rubbed and defeatured by the twin hurricanes named Just Do It and Just Say No" (140).

170. Foucault, *L'Herméneutique du sujet,* 242; *Hermeneutics of the Subject,* 252 (translation once again altered). For an exemplary analysis with specific reference to HIV/AIDS, which emphasizes large-scale social processes but understands their direct relevance to individual choices and practices, see Samuel R. Friedman, Susan C. Kippax, Nancy Phaswana-Mafuya, Diana Rossi, and Christy E. Newman, "Emerging Future Issues in HIV/AIDS Social Research," *AIDS,* 20.7 (April 24, 2006), 959–65.

Acknowledgments

Earlier versions of this essay were written to be delivered as public lectures or keynote addresses at the following conferences: "The Ends of Sexuality: Pleasure and Danger in the New Millennium," Northwestern University (April 2003); "Sexuality After Foucault," University of Manchester (November 2003); "Foucault y la sexualidad: Celebración a 20 años de su muerte," Universidad Nacional Autónoma de México (August 2004); The Fourth Annual National Sexuality Resource Center Summer Institute on Sexuality, Society, and Health, San Francisco State University (July 2005); "Sexuality Out of Place," Earlham College (March–April 2006); "FUTURE*QUEER," University College, Dublin (June–July 2006); and "Desprenderse de la psicopatología," Semana de la école lacanienne de psychanalyse 2006, Mexico City (August 2006). I wish to thank the organizers of those events for giving me an opportunity to present my work and test my thinking, as well as the audiences for their questions and challenges, which have contributed significantly to the final form of my essay. I also wish to thank Jill and Tobin Siebers and my colleagues at the University of Michigan in Ann Arbor, who provided bracing and constructive critiques of several drafts, and audiences at Cornell University, Trinity College, Brown University, Wayne State University, and the Centro Cultural Rector Ricardo Rojas at the Universidad de Buenos Aires, for their stimulating responses.

My work has been generously, enthusiastically supported by the University of Michigan. Since 2001, the College of Literature, Science, and the Arts has given me two leaves from teaching, in addition to a sabbatical, and the

Institute for the Humanities awarded me a John Rich Professorship and Michigan Faculty Fellowship. For this material assistance, and the immaterial faith in my work that it expresses, I am immensely grateful.

I have profited enormously from discussions with Barry Adam, Jean Allouch, Brent Armendinger, Alex Bacon, Susana Bercovich, Lauren Berlant, Leo Bersani, Manuel Hernández García, Ellis Hanson, Peter Hegarty, Trevor Hoppe, Myra Jehlen, Susan Kippax, Heather Love, Michele Morales, Paul Morrison, Suraj Patel, Kane Race, the late Eric Rofes, Ron Stall, Jack Tocco, Greg Tomso, Valerie Traub, Carol Vernallis, and Marie Ymonet, nearly all of whom read earlier versions of this essay, provided me with rigorous, searching critiques of it, and saved me from many embarrassing errors. I have also benefitted from two anonymous evaluations of the manuscript of this book by readers for the University of Michigan Press. Alison Mackeen, my editor at the Press, provided me with a superbly astute and tactful critique of the penultimate draft. I wish to thank LaMont Egle and, especially, Chad Thomas for help in locating sources. I am particularly grateful to Richard J. Wolitski, Acting Director, Division of HIV/AIDS Prevention at the National Center for HIV/AIDS, Viral Hepatitis, STD, and TB Prevention at the Centers for Disease Control and Prevention, for providing me with information about the scope of the HIV/AIDS epidemic in the United States. None of the persons mentioned above should be presumed to agree with any of the claims advanced in this book.

I owe a special debt of gratitude to Michael Warner, who asked, nearly fifteen years ago, "What do queers want?"; who has been willing to debate the issues with me ever since; and who has helped me with this work despite being the principal object of its critique. He continues, as I hope will be obvious from what I say about him here, to be an inspiration.

D. M. H.
Ann Arbor
December 10, 2006
October 6, 2008

Appendix

UNSAFE:
WHY GAY MEN
ARE HAVING RISKY SEX
Michael Warner

Village Voice, January 31, 1995

In flyblown offices near Union Square, men arrive, fill out a questionnaire, and take an HIV test. Then they sit down with a counselor to talk about their sex lives. Have you rimmed another man in the past three months? What were your thoughts when you asked him to fuck you?

These men are part of Project ACHIEVE, a study launched by the New York Blood Center over a year ago. Its main purpose is to identify a population for future vaccine trials. But in the process of interviewing over 450 gay men every three months, Project ACHIEVE is yielding probably the most reliable picture anyone has of risky sex among HIV-negative gay men in New York.

Investigators wanted to know: Have you had anal sex in the last three months, without using a condom, with another man who was either positive or of unknown status? The response was alarming enough: 20 per cent said they'd been fucked unsafely, 25 per cent that they had fucked someone else without a condom. But these figures show why statistics are misleading about sex. The interviewers discovered that many men were having partial or momentary insertions they did not consider to be "anal sex." When these encounters are included, the numbers rise to 30 per cent (fucked) and 38 per cent (fucking).

This is no random sample; the project recruits negative men, and involvement in it implies awareness of AIDS and a conscious gay or bi identity. If even these men are turning to unsafe sex, the numbers may be higher among gays as a whole.

Similar figures are coming in from other studies. One group of researchers, surveying gay men in 16 small cities from upstate New York to West Virginia and Montana, found that about a third of the men reported fucking without condoms in the previous two months. A soon-to-be-released study of young men in San Francisco found rates of new infection nearly four times what they were in 1987.

Researchers at Columbia University focused on younger gay men in New York. They recently projected that the infection rate among gay men is likely to remain stable for a long time, with a slight decline over 40 years. But they add that if the men they interviewed had underreported their unsafe contacts by as little as one per year, the disease will become even more widespread than it already is, with infection rates for some age groups rising to over 60 per cent in the next decade. The epidemic, they conclude, presents one of the classic disaster scenarios of game theory: An increase in unprotected sex may only slightly raise the risk for individuals (since that risk is high already), but if everyone were to take that gamble at once, infection rates would explode.

Studies such as these have led many to speak of a coming "second wave of AIDS." But we may only now be noticing what has been there for a long time: that safer sex is easer to adopt in the short run than to sustain. And we may be noticing this for a simple reason: Since the 1993 Berlin AIDS conference, which doused hopes for an imminent cure and dashed faith in drugs like AZT, it has become increasingly clear that the AIDS epidemic is likely to last for the rest of our lives. Slogans like "Be here for the cure!" are starting to ring hollow. Under these conditions, surrounded by positive friends and lovers, negative gay men face a new kind of challenge, one few outside our milieu can understand.

What makes some men fuck without protection when they know about the dangers, when they have access to condoms, when they have practiced safe sex for years, even when they have long involvement in AIDS activism—in short, when they "know better"? The question is shocking, incomprehensible. I know. When I had an unsafe encounter last winter, I spooked myself blank.

Afterward, I thought: good. Be afraid. Be very afraid. It will keep you safer in the future. I checked the calendar to see when three months would pass. (The body can take that long—some specialists say up to six months—to produce antibodies to HIV.) It seemed, to use America's Favorite Cliché, a wake-up call.

Some men think they're immune, because they're too young, or because they're not bottoms, or because the other guy just looks healthy. But I was not that kind of fool. The city's Department of Health has never bothered to do the studies that San Francisco has, but the best estimates are that about 50 per cent of gay men my age in New York have HIV. If you have only one partner, the chances are pretty good that he has it.

The odds occurred to me at the time, in a kind of instant calculus that was not even recognizable as thinking, much less as making a decision. The quality of consciousness was more like impulse shoplifting. When I talked to my best friends about the episode, I mentioned only how explosive the sex had been; not that it was unsafe. I recoiled so much from what I had done that it seemed to be not my choice at all. A mystery, I thought. A monster did it.

The next time I saw the same man, we went back to his apartment again. I thought to myself to take precautions, but I could tell by the heady thrill that my monster was in charge. Even scarier than the risk itself was the realization that shame and fear had not been enough to keep me safe. Suddenly I had to think about why I wanted risky sex, knowing that the danger was part of the attraction. In the vast industry of AIDS education and prevention, I knew of nothing that would help me answer this question.

Safer sex has been around since 1983, and the basic priorities of prevention have changed little since then: Get the information out and make it attractive. But over and over I hear the same thing from prevention workers: information itself is no longer doing the job. "Everybody's grandmother knows about anal sex and latex," one activist said to me. The Minority Task Force on AIDS sends out health educators like Juan Olmedo to cruisy spots. They go to bars and cruising spots in parks to pass out condoms and lube. Their aim is to reach men who aren't immersed in gay culture, who spend little time in information-rich white neighborhoods. But most of the men they find there already know more than the basics of safe sex. Says Olmedo, "People look at the condoms we give them and say, 'Oh, I thought nonoxynol-9 isn't supposed to be good for you any more.'"

Prevention activists have gone back to the drawing board. They convened an HIV-prevention summit in Dallas last June, with federal help. As a follow-up, 16 prevention-related organizations in New York held an open community meeting on November 16. Not surprisingly, it produced more talk than action. Some of the talk is new: "harm reduction," "self-efficacy," "negotiated safety," "stages of change," "maintenance." But everyone seems to be waiting for a much bigger New Idea. "We need a prevention movement," says Mike Isbell, a policy director at Gay Men's Health Crisis. And no one yet knows what that would look like.

There is also plenty of disagreement about how "unsafe" should be defined. The biggest arguments involve oral sex. The San Francisco Young Men's Health Study is typical of much research in concluding that oral sex alone had "no association" with positivity. The Multicenter AIDS Cohort Study (MACS) found that oral transmission was "possible, albeit rare." Other specialists argue that these statistics may understate the risk by attributing some oral transmission to anal sex. At any rate, it has been documented that HIV can be spread through oral sex.

The debate gets very technical, but ultimately reduces to a question on which no one is an expert: How much risk is acceptable? For years the major prevention organizations—including GMHC—and government agencies said none. They classified oral sex without latex, even without ejaculation, as unsafe. By most accounts, a significant number of gay men—like most heterosexuals—have simply ignored the advice, or have set a goal of safer rather than absolutely safe sex.

On top of these disputes, government remains reluctant to fund research into infection trends, risk, and prevention. The now notorious *Sex in America* survey was initially conceived as research to help AIDS prevention; after its funding was gutted by congressional Republicans who feared a new Kinsey Report, the study was so reduced that it finally interviewed fewer than 50 gay or bisexual men. Content restrictions are still in place for some federally funded prevention; even materials for the summit in Dallas had to be vetted for anything that might "promote homosexuality."

In New York, cases among injection-drug users have outnumbered cases among men who have sex with men every year since 1989. Still, the state's AIDS Institute issued 160 prevention contracts for the year ending June 1994; only 16 targeted men who have sex with men. Some local governments, such as San Francisco, have tried to fill the gap. But in New York City, very little has been done to find out what gay men are actually doing or how widespread HIV might be.

Until recently, the future looked a little brighter. The Clinton administration had indicated a willingness to relax content restrictions. The Centers for Disease Control had launched a massive project to give community activists a say in funding priorities. And the New York AIDS Institute had announced a new grant of $2.45 million for prevention programs targeting gay men and lesbians. But then came the election, and right-wing budget cutters go with gay-targeted prevention like Crisco and condoms: fatally.

Meanwhile, the straight press, learning of the "second wave," has been eager to pin the rap on gay men. The press has always loved to interpret gay men's desires as pathological: you have a tragic shortage of self-esteem, you've given up, you're irresponsible. And for gay writers there is no easier way to get attention from the tabs than to scapegoat queer sex, as Randy Shilts and Larry Kramer proved the first time around. The second wave has produced its own fraternity of gay critics. *New York Newsday* columnist Gabriel Rotello has described sex clubs as "the killing fields of AIDS." And the *Daily News* has drawn a touching moral from the prevention crisis: it is time for gay men to promote "love and meaningful relationships, instead of backroom dalliances."

But not a single study has shown that the second wave of AIDS can be traced to sex clubs. Most risk happens in the bedroom, not the back room. One Australian study of unsafe sex among young men found that over 70 per cent of these incidents had taken place at home, with public parks and toilets at about 10 per cent. In one San Francisco study of unsafe sex, researchers asked men what their reasons had been for taking risks. Most said simply that they had been turned on. But many said that they had been "in love," precisely what the *News* recommends.

When we talk about gay men having unsafe sex, then, we aren't referring to coked-up, narcissistically impaired bingers in unlit back rooms (as if such people were unworthy of being taken seriously). This is why Carlos Cordero, outreach coordinator at Project ACHIEVE, worries about putting the findings in context. "If we just release our figures about unsafe sex, people are going to say: 'Look how foolish gay men are.' If we marry the figures with some knowledge about the reasons for having unsafe sex, people will say: 'I've been there. I've been depressed. I've been in love.' Sometimes," Cordero adds, "there's no explanation."

Unlike sex per se, unsafe sex requires two people, one negative and one positive. But prevention studies have hardly ever focused on the dynamic between gay partners. "People try to push boundaries," says Cordero. "Let me see how far I can get you to go with me. If I rub my dick up against your hole, that's a way of saying, 'Let's play the '70s game. We won't go all the way; just a little bit.'" Cordero attributes much of this dynamic to what he calls "top mentality": men mistakenly perceive themselves not to be at risk as tops. "Bottom mentality," on the other hand, means wanting not to have to deal with negotiation over safety; it's the job of the top to be responsible for that. But tops may be thinking it's the job of the bottom.

Often the decision is made by the context. "You're more relaxed in your own home," Cordero says. "The wine's flowing, the candle's burning, hopefully the wax is getting on your body. That's when a lot of people take chances." In the Latino community, says Cordero, the high value on romance and intimacy means that condoms, which connote promiscuity, are suspect. "When you meet someone you like, the condoms are going to go out the window. For the same reason, there is a suspicion that anyone who brings out a condom must be promiscuous and positive. There's a disincentive both to condoms and to disclosure."

For many positive men, the solution is to sort out anonymous encounters, in which safer sex can make HIV-status moot, and more personal ones, where early disclosure will be important in the development of trust.

This ethic has its own pitfalls. Richard Elovich, who runs programs at GMHC for gay men with drug and alcohol problems, finds that a common theme in the groups is what he calls "werewolf anxiety": the burden of secrecy and shame that positive men carry when they didn't disclose at first, perhaps in a casual encounter that later became more serious; or when they do disclose and the other man's reaction makes even a safe, casual encounter difficult. It's no wonder, then, that many positive men decide to talk later or not at all.

In the case of my own unsafe encounters last winter, many of these undiscussed issues were at play. Why, for example, had the other guy wanted to be fucked without a condom? I think I pretended not to ask myself this question, knowing the simplest theory: because he was already positive and wasn't worried about being infected. Usually, men who know they are positive will either tell you their status or take on themselves the burden of keeping things safe. He hadn't. But he would have been quite reasonable to think, since I went along, either that I was making my own decisions or that I, too, was already positive and wasn't worried about reinfection.

There were other possibilities, consolation theories for me. Plenty of men, usually young, want unprotected sex because they trust the people they're with to be negative. But this was no ingenue, and he had a collection of sex toys to prove it. Of course, it was also possible that, like me, he was negative or didn't know his status, and was simply willing to take a risk. These other possibilities, I now understand, preserved the level of uncertainty I wanted in order to take a risk; I dwelt on them just long enough to think that I didn't know what I thought I knew I was doing.

Gay men are so aware of the language of responsibility, guilt, and shame—remember homophobia?—that we go to great lengths to avoid it. Richard Elovich thinks this may be one reason for the link between unsafe sex and what is euphemistically called "substance abuse." "When people get high and have unprotected sex," he asks, "which comes first? People assume that drugs lead to unsafe sex. But often the desire is there from the beginning. Men get high or drunk because they can't acknowledge that desire, or because they want someone else to be in control, or because they just don't want to make a choice." Call it the poppers effect: you give yourself a chance to swoon. Talking dirty and going to sex clubs may work the same way. Without exactly causing unsafe sex, they may be contexts that gay men seek in order to escape their own self-monitoring.

The appeal of queer sex, for many, lies in its ability to violate the responsibilizing frames of good, right-thinking people. AIDS education, in contrast, often calls for people to affirm life and see sex as a healthy expression of self-esteem and respect for others. One campaign from the San Francisco AIDS Foundation urges men to treat sex the way you might buy municipal bonds: "Playing it safe, making a plan, and sticking to it." Most efforts to encourage us to take care of ourselves through safer sex also invite us to pretend that our only desire is to be proper and good. Abjection continues to be our dirty secret.

The queerness that is repressed in this view may be finding expression in risk. Sex has long been associated with death, in part because of its sublimity. Even Kant—Mr. Responsibility himself—understood it: there is no sublimity without danger, without the scary ability to imagine ourselves and everything we hold dear, at least for a moment, as expendable.

In this context, the pursuit of dangerous sex is not as simple as mere thrill seeking, or self-destructiveness. It may represent deep and mostly unconscious thinking about desire and the conditions that make life worthwhile.

Critic and activist Douglas Crimp believes that, for these reasons, the emphasis on self-esteem, which many are promoting on the model of 12-step programs, may be counterproductive: "Most people only have pop psychology for thinking about sex. Only if you can acknowledge that you have an unconscious can you admit doing self-destructive things without just feeling guilty. We all fail to realize how powerful the unconscious is." The trouble with the pop psychology of self-esteem is what it fails to acknowledge: "It's your self that wants the risk."

Positive thinking may also prevent us from seeing a major motive for risk taking: a deep identification with positive men, ambivalence about survival, and the rejection of normal life. Walt Odets, a San Francisco therapist and prevention activist, argues that AIDS prevention cannot deal with new realities until it takes into account the peculiar dilemmas of negative men. In a forthcoming book called *Being HIV-Negative,* Odets suggests that people who live outside the cities hardest hit by HIV can scarcely imagine the damage to one's sense of identity. In the eyes of the straight world, gay still means AIDS; to come out is to come into the epidemic. More to the point, our own lives are bound up with positive friends and lovers to such a degree that many gay men are unwilling to say openly that they are negative. It sounds like an affront, a betrayal of the men with whom we identify, and in comparison with whom our troubles will seem trivial.

From treatment activism to magazines like *Poz* and *Diseased Pariah News,* and the work of artists like Bill T. Jones and David Wojnarowicz, positive men have developed a culture of articulacy about mortality and the expectations of "normal life." When negative men identify with positive men, they are not just operating out of survivor guilt. They are staking their interests with that culture and taking as their own its priorities, its mordant humor, its heightened tempo, its long view on the world.

This is one of the major differences between the '80s and the '90s: being positive has become an identity. No longer associated directly with sickness, positive men often remain asymptomatic for years. Unsafe sex has changed in meaning as a result. When a negative man has unsafe sex today, it may mean not so much a gamble with the banalities of infection and disease as a way of trying on the cultural identity of the HIV-positive.

Odets writes that negative men often try to live "as a dying man does, without a belief in or sense of responsibility to the future, existing within the scope and scale of a life that may end any day. This form of life often feels plausible and defensible only if the man actually has HIV, and the 'incentive' to have it may be enhanced by the sometimes liberating nature of such lives." In this line of thinking Odets leads us well beyond the platitudes of those who want us simply to be more life-affirming, have higher self-esteem. Both the so-called mainstream of American culture and gay activists who insist on optimism, he contends, "conspire to 'normalize' the epidemic by denying the radical form of life it has created for many gay men."

The identification of negative men with the culture of positive men can be liberating if it cultivates this radical form of life. But it will be crippling if negative men cannot even acknowledge their distinctiveness, if they live through the contradictions of life with AIDS simply by denying them. And if the erotic practice of risk supplants thinking about their way of life.

At the New York meeting in November, activist Carmen Vasquez tried to counter the tendency to despair by drawing on the traditions of ethnic identity—in her case, Puerto Rican. "I know something about survival," she said at the close of her remarks, to great applause: "ask me." Despair, she pointed out, may be more keenly felt by the privileged, who had higher expectations for their lives.

But for gay men living in the context of AIDS, ethnic identity may not be solace enough. "I'm torn between Carmen's vision of struggle and survival, and white gay men's experience of despair," says Colin Robinson of Gay Men of African Descent. "To be honest, I find the despair easier to understand. You have to have a cohort that you're surviving with." And as Douglas Crimp points out, despair is hardly foreign to minority communities. "You could say that 14-year-olds with guns are like gay men having unsafe sex; there's despair on both sides. Cornel West writes eloquently of the nihilism that has taken over parts of African American culture, where the hard thing is to get people thinking about survival again. I think we're facing something similar."

Despair is not always failed nerve. It's possible to have high self-esteem and still be unhappy with the world. "It isn't just that we don't feel good about ourselves," says Crimp. "We don't feel good. And there are reasons for that. After all this epidemic, all this hatred from the right, all this loss, we're demoralized. We don't say that because we think despair is defeat. Unsafe sex is partly about just not wanting to deal with this whole issue anymore." It may also be the closest many can come to asking out loud: under what conditions is life worth surviving for?

"My own survival," writes social theorist Zygmunt Bauman, "cannot be savoured otherwise than as a macabre privilege over the others, less fortunate. Yet these others may be, and more often than not are, the very meaning of my existence—the uppermost value which makes my life worth living; the very sense of being alive." If surviving AIDS means surviving all your positive friends and lovers, is the *you* that survives someone that you can imagine? "After all," Bauman goes on, as though he were thinking of gay men in the world of AIDS, "I want to survive mostly because the thought of all that communication, intercourse, loving, being loved—all that grinding suddenly to a halt is so unbearable."

If a new prevention movement comes about, it will have a lot to do. But there can hardly be a more basic need than for gay men to develop a better culture of discussion. Unsafe sex is shoved out of mind, out of sight. As Richard Elovich put it at the New York meeting: "We haven't created the spaces where gay men can be honest with each other, and that's the beginning of harm reduction. If I can't talk honestly about what it means to me to have someone's dick up my butt or to have someone come in my mouth, I can't think through what it would cost me to give it up."

When I began to see that my own ventures into unsafe sex were not random accidents, that they were the expression of desires and circumstances that I shared with other queer men, but could not easily discuss with anyone, I decided to try a difficult experiment. I called the man I'd had sex with on those occasions last winter. We had developed a strong bond in the time we saw each other. And I thought we could talk freely. After waiting for several months, I had finally taken a new HIV test and learned that I was still, through no virtue of my own, negative.

I left messages for Mike. They went unreturned. Finally the word came back: Mike had died of AIDS only a month after I last saw him, healthy and beautiful as ever.

The best I can do for Mike is damaged grieving, over the noise of conversations we didn't have, conversations I helped to postpone so as not to think about exactly this— or rather to think about this loss of an already necrotic world only in the practice of risk.

"The safest way to not get HIV," says Odets, "is never to touch another human being. So if someone is anxious, start there. But then you have to ask: what do you want to do? How important is it to you? Who are you? What do you want your life to be about?"

Text design by Jillian Downey
Typesetting by Delmastype, Ann Arbor, Michigan
Font: Adobe Garamond

Claude Garamond's sixteenth-century types were modeled on those of Venetian printers from the end of the previous century. Adobe designer Robert Slimbach based his Adobe Garamond roman typefaces on the original Garamond types, and based his italics on types by Robert Granjon, a contemporary of Garamond's. Slimbach's Adobe Garamond was released in 1989.

—courtesy www.adobe.com